INVITATION
TO A
Royal
Wedding

5

The Lord Chamber

The Queen and The D

....

INVITATION TO A

to the

His Royal Highnes

The Lady

in St. Pau

on Wednesday, 29th

An answer is requested to the Lord Chamberlain,
St. James's Palace, London, S.W.1.

R

is Commanded by

of Edinburgh to invite

....

Royal Wedding

....

riage of

he Prince of Wales

na Spencer

Cathedral

, 1981 at 11.00 a.m.

Dress: Uniform, Morning Dress
or Lounge Suit.

THE WEDDING ROUTE

The route taken by the carriage processions from Buckingham Palace (and in the case of the bride's procession, from Clarence House) along the Mall, through Trafalgar Square, the Strand, Fleet Street and up Ludgate Hill to St Paul's Cathedral is lined by approximately 2,800 Police officers and 1,000 Servicemen, representing all three services:

From Buckingham Palace to Admiralty Arch: The Brigade of Guards.

From Admiralty Arch to half way down the Strand: The Royal Navy (The Ministry of Defence has said that this is "so that Nelson can keep an eye on his boys").

From the Strand to Temple Bar: The Royal Air Force.

In the City: The Army, mainly Territorials.

To add to the splendour and pageantry of the occasion, all coachmen, postillions and footmen involved in the processions wear State Liveries, except the postillions of the carriage in which the bridegroom travels to St Paul's and returns to Buckingham Palace with his bride. These wear Ascot Liveries of scarlet, purple and gold jackets, similar to the Queen's Racing Colours. The coachmen in State Livery wear scarlet and gold frock-coats with scarlet plush knee-breeches, pink silk stockings, gold-buckled shoes, wigs and tricorn hats with ostrich feathers. Postillions wear scarlet and gold jackets, wigs and caps, buckskin breeches and top boots.

Buckingham Palace, the starting point for the carriage processions of the Queen and Prince Charles, became the principal residence of the sovereign on the accession of Queen Victoria in 1837.

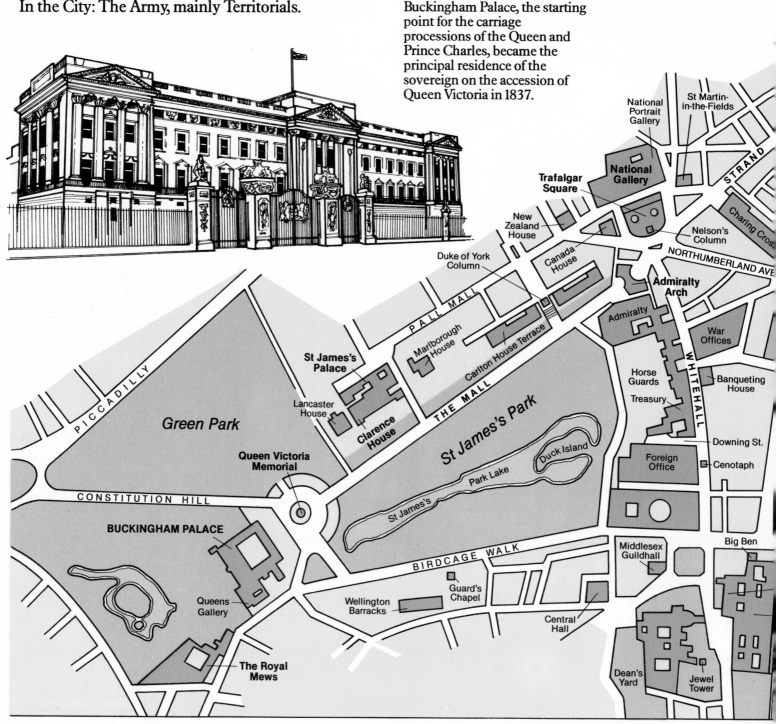

THE WEDDING ROUTE

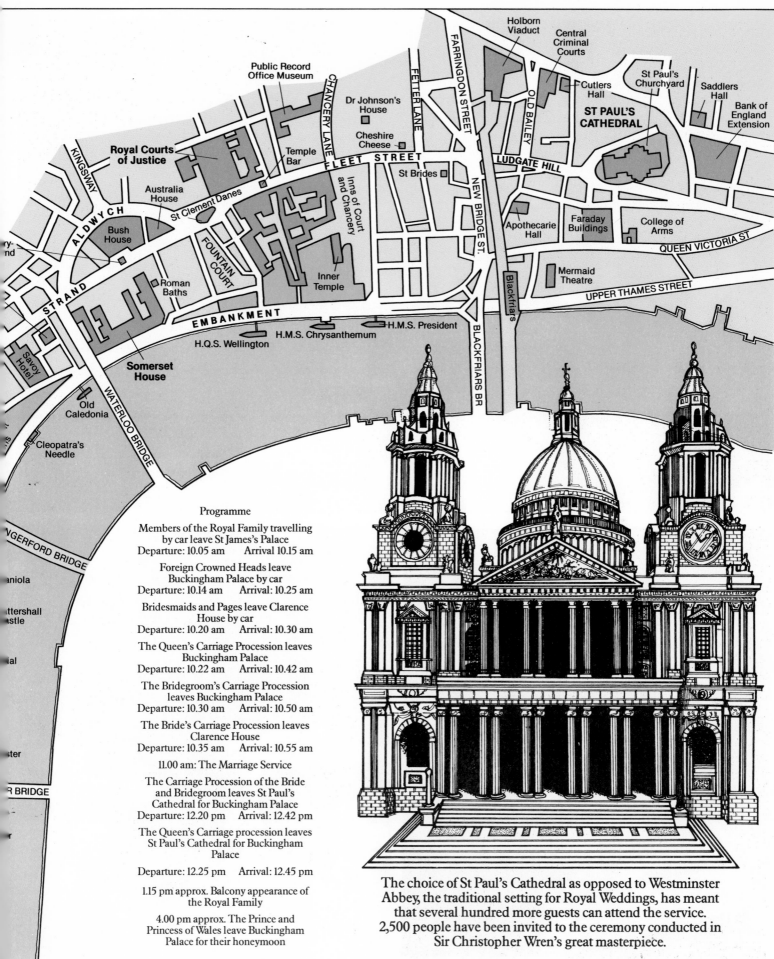

Holborn Viaduct
Central Criminal Courts
Farringdon Street
Old Bailey
Cutlers Hall
St Paul's Churchyard
Saddlers Hall
Bank of England Extension

Public Record Office Museum
Chancery Lane
Fetter Lane
ST PAUL'S CATHEDRAL

Dr Johnson's House
Cheshire Cheese

Royal Courts of Justice
Temple Bar
FLEET STREET
St Brides
LUDGATE HILL

Kingsway
Australia House
St Clement Danes
Inns of Court and Chancery
New Bridge St.
Apothecarie Hall
Faraday Buildings
College of Arms

Aldwych
Bush House
FOUNTAIN COURT
Blackfriars
QUEEN VICTORIA ST.

Strand
Roman Baths
Inner Temple
Mermaid Theatre
UPPER THAMES STREET

EMBANKMENT
H.Q.S. Wellington
H.M.S. Chrysanthemum
H.M.S. President
BLACKFRIARS BR.

Savoy Hotel
Somerset House

Old Caledonia
WATERLOO BRIDGE

Cleopatra's Needle

HUNGERFORD BRIDGE

aniola

ttershall astle

ster

R BRIDGE

Programme

Members of the Royal Family travelling by car leave St James's Palace
Departure: 10.05 am   Arrival 10.15 am

Foreign Crowned Heads leave Buckingham Palace by car
Departure: 10.14 am   Arrival: 10.25 am

Bridesmaids and Pages leave Clarence House by car
Departure: 10.20 am   Arrival: 10.30 am

The Queen's Carriage Procession leaves Buckingham Palace
Departure: 10.22 am   Arrival: 10.42 am

The Bridegroom's Carriage Procession leaves Buckingham Palace
Departure: 10.30 am   Arrival: 10.50 am

The Bride's Carriage Procession leaves Clarence House
Departure: 10.35 am   Arrival: 10.55 am

11.00 am: The Marriage Service

The Carriage Procession of the Bride and Bridegroom leaves St Paul's Cathedral for Buckingham Palace
Departure: 12.20 pm   Arrival: 12.42 pm

The Queen's Carriage procession leaves St Paul's Cathedral for Buckingham Palace

Departure: 12.25 pm   Arrival: 12.45 pm

1.15 pm approx. Balcony appearance of the Royal Family

4.00 pm approx. The Prince and Princess of Wales leave Buckingham Palace for their honeymoon

The choice of St Paul's Cathedral as opposed to Westminster Abbey, the traditional setting for Royal Weddings, has meant that several hundred more guests can attend the service. 2,500 people have been invited to the ceremony conducted in Sir Christopher Wren's great masterpiece.

A Marriage of Heart and Mind, Music and Faith

FOREWORD

This is a special Royal Wedding. The place is special. The last Royal Wedding in St Paul's was the ill-fated marriage of Prince Arthur to Catherine of Aragon in 1501. The decision of the Prince of Wales to ask to be married in St Paul's, now very much the Peoples' Cathedral, was a surprise and a change of precedent. There is an openness about St Paul's; its design, its situation at the heart of London, its survival through plague, fire and bombardment, its vocation to lay the gospel out before the crowds, all give it a special role among historic churches which are both holy and challenging.

St Paul's speaks of that 'other country' recalled in some words especially chosen by the Prince himself to be sung at the end of his wedding:

"And there's another country, I've heard of long ago,
Most dear to them that love her, most great to them that know;
We may not count her armies, we may not see her King;
Her fortress is a faithful heart, her pride is suffering;
And soul by soul and silently her shining bounds increase,
And her ways are ways of gentleness and all her paths are peace."

The Churches have responded to this special wedding. For the first time, the leaders of the different branches of the Church: Anglican, Free Church and Roman Catholic, will take the Service together. For the first time, a lay Free Churchman, Mr Speaker, who is a member of the Welsh Methodist Church, will read the lesson – the supreme words about love in St Paul's letter to the Corinthians, Chapter 13. The Archbishop will preach, no doubt as directly as the Prince himself preached in St Paul's two years ago on the tragic occasion of Earl Mountbatten's Memorial Service. An ordained deaconess will process robed among the clergy. Words derived from prayers ancient and modern, Pre-Reformation 1662, 1928 and 1980 will be used in the Service. The solemn gesture by which the bridegroom lets the ring rest on the bride's finger, saying as he does: "In the name of the Father, and of the Son and of the Holy Spirit" has been used in marriages for more than 600 years. So historic disagreements are being transcended, and the Service itself points to a new unity in the future.

The Dome of St Paul's will resound as never before to choirs and orchestras, hymns and trumpets, reflecting the Prince of Wales' love of music and his skill as a musician. On this occasion, Sir David Willcocks, Director of the Royal College of Music, assists Christopher Dearnley, the Cathedral Organist who plays brilliantly week by week for services in St Paul's as well as responding to invitations from round the world. The Cathedral Choir, the Choir of the Chapel Royal, the London Bach Choir and the augmented Covent Garden Orchestra are combining to lead the singing of the congregation as well as the anthems, some specially composed. The soprano soloist, Kiri Te Kanawa, will sing during the signing of the register, just before the bride and bridegroom process from the altar to the street outside down that great royal carpet, all 160 yards of it.

So the place, service and music are special but the purpose is the same as that in every wedding, religious or civil, in every culture and country. A wedding is a meeting of friends who by their presence or prayers affirm that in a world where there is so much bad news, here is an event winged with joy – a new human relationship based on fidelity, hope and love.

Dean of St Paul's

The Dean left and the choir under the direction of Barry Rose have a special commitment to ensuring that the wedding is a joyous occasion.

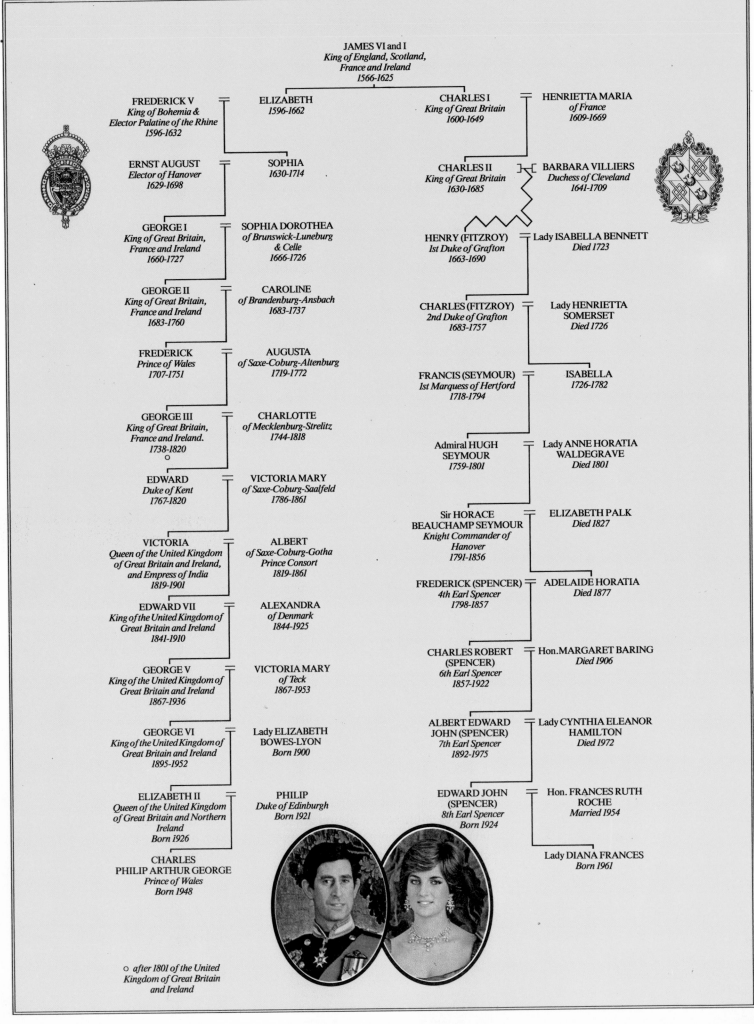

JAMES VI and I
*King of England, Scotland,
France and Ireland*
1566-1625

FREDERICK V
*King of Bohemia &
Elector Palatine of the Rhine
1596-1632*

ELIZABETH
1596-1662

CHARLES I
*King of Great Britain
1600-1649*

HENRIETTA MARIA
*of France
1609-1669*

ERNST AUGUST
*Elector of Hanover
1629-1698*

SOPHIA
1630-1714

CHARLES II
*King of Great Britain
1630-1685*

BARBARA VILLIERS
*Duchess of Cleveland
1641-1709*

GEORGE I
*King of Great Britain,
France and Ireland
1660-1727*

SOPHIA DOROTHEA
*of Brunswick-Luneburg
& Celle
1666-1726*

HENRY (FITZROY)
*1st Duke of Grafton
1663-1690*

Lady ISABELLA BENNETT
Died 1723

GEORGE II
*King of Great Britain,
France and Ireland
1683-1760*

CAROLINE
*of Brandenburg-Ansbach
1683-1737*

CHARLES (FITZROY)
*2nd Duke of Grafton
1683-1757*

Lady HENRIETTA
SOMERSET
Died 1726

FREDERICK
*Prince of Wales
1707-1751*

AUGUSTA
*of Saxe-Coburg-Altenburg
1719-1772*

FRANCIS (SEYMOUR)
*1st Marquess of Hertford
1718-1794*

ISABELLA
1726-1782

GEORGE III
*King of Great Britain,
France and Ireland.
1738-1820*
o

CHARLOTTE
*of Mecklenburg-Strelitz
1744-1818*

Admiral HUGH
SEYMOUR
1759-1801

Lady ANNE HORATIA
WALDEGRAVE
Died 1801

EDWARD
*Duke of Kent
1767-1820*

VICTORIA MARY
*of Saxe-Coburg-Saalfeld
1786-1861*

Sir HORACE
BEAUCHAMP SEYMOUR
*Knight Commander of
Hanover
1791-1856*

ELIZABETH PALK
Died 1827

VICTORIA
*Queen of the United Kingdom
of Great Britain and Ireland,
and Empress of India
1819-1901*

ALBERT
*of Saxe-Coburg-Gotha
Prince Consort
1819-1861*

FREDERICK (SPENCER)
*4th Earl Spencer
1798-1857*

ADELAIDE HORATIA
Died 1877

EDWARD VII
*King of the United Kingdom of
Great Britain and Ireland
1841-1910*

ALEXANDRA
*of Denmark
1844-1925*

CHARLES ROBERT
(SPENCER)
*6th Earl Spencer
1857-1922*

Hon. MARGARET BARING
Died 1906

GEORGE V
*King of the United Kingdom of
Great Britain and Ireland
1867-1936*

VICTORIA MARY
*of Teck
1867-1953*

ALBERT EDWARD
JOHN (SPENCER)
*7th Earl Spencer
1892-1975*

Lady CYNTHIA ELEANOR
HAMILTON
Died 1972

GEORGE VI
*King of the United Kingdom of
Great Britain and Ireland
1895-1952*

Lady ELIZABETH
BOWES-LYON
Born 1900

EDWARD JOHN
(SPENCER)
*8th Earl Spencer
Born 1924*

Hon. FRANCES RUTH
ROCHE
Married 1954

ELIZABETH II
*Queen of the United Kingdom
of Great Britain and Northern
Ireland
Born 1926*

PHILIP
*Duke of Edinburgh
Born 1921*

Lady DIANA FRANCES
Born 1961

CHARLES
PHILIP ARTHUR GEORGE
*Prince of Wales
Born 1948*

o *after 1801 of the United
Kingdom of Great Britain
and Ireland*

12

THE COURTSHIP OF A PRINCE OF WALES

The announcement of the betrothal of the Prince of Wales to Lady Diana Spencer on 24th February 1981 heralded an event which has captured the eyes and the imagination of the world and its media in a possibly unprecedented furore of public interest and involvement. For many journalists and photographers alike it represented the joyful conclusion to weeks of playing the not always enjoyable game of "hunt the Prince of Wales" and more particularly, "spot Lady Diana". The public reaction was on the whole that of a very natural human joy that an exceedingly popular young man should at last have found someone with whom to share his life, tinged with that special mingling of respect and affection which the British public still reserve for their Royal Family. If the press at times overstepped the mark in an attempt to report the details of the "Royal Romance" to the world at large, then their efforts can only really be justified in terms of an apparently insatiable public interest in anything to do with the Royal Family but particularly in anything which shows its members to be "human".

Significantly it was discussion of the official title of King George VI's elder daughter which provided one of the early examples of the interest taken in the Royal Family by the popular newspapers and their readers. The Princess Elizabeth was never made Princess of Wales as some considered she should be but comprehensive newspaper speculation about the title for their future Queen was a contributory factor in the vital process of humanizing the institutional

The Prince of Wales' Coat of Arms: a version of the Royal Arms surrounded by the Garter, with the Prince of Wales' Feathers and Welsh Dragon embellishing the motto Ich Dien – "I Serve".

monarchy. The advent of cinema, radio and the motor car served to make individual members of the Royal Family more accessible and better known, and by the end of the Second World War the monarch had been transformed from a profile on a postage stamp or a coin of the realm – at most a waving silhouette on a distant balcony – into a three-dimensional living person. It is hardly surprising therefore, that on the birth of Prince Charles Philip Arthur George on 14th November 1948, editors and columnists began to proffer all the well-intentioned but unsolicited advice they believed their readership would like to see given to England's number one family. The tide of interest could not be halted. By the time Prince Charles had reached the ripe old age of four, one magazine editor, who must be commended at least for taking the initiative, had already published the first list of likely ladies he might one day marry.

Throughout the Prince's boyhood and teenage years the list was to be constantly altered and amended as first one girl, then another, was, frequently for no tangible reason, either eliminated or raised to the position of "favourite". The criteria for judgement ranged from social to astrological suitability (Lady Diana born under Cancer

has been cited as a perfect match for the Scorpio Prince) and the name of the game varied from "Prince Charming's search for his fairy-tale Princess" to a "Royal Miss World Competition" and even to a kind of matrimonial Grand National with reference to such betting terms as "favourites" and "outsiders". The "odds" on a Royal Wedding taking place in the near future increased when Prince Charles left the rigorous confines of Gordonstoun for the more liberal academic and social world of Trinity College, Cambridge, and grew out of all proportion when he reached his thirtieth birthday. His admission in November 1975 that he thought thirty was a good age for a man to marry no doubt appeared harmless to him at the time; three years later he may well have regretted his remark.

Commenting on his own reaction to press coverage, Prince Charles has claimed, "I have layers to protect me", and it is a credit to both parties that relations between the Palace and the press are generally very good. During his courtship the Prince made a sport out of foxing newspaper camera men, going to all kinds of lengths to ensure that he and Lady Diana were not photographed together before their engagement. The first real pictures were in fact the official ones taken on the terrace at the back of Buckingham Palace on the day of the announcement but to secure their privacy prior to that, the Prince and Lady Diana were reduced to subterfuge. On one occasion Lady Diana was even forced to escape the cameras by lying in the back of a Landrover covered with a blanket.

THE COURTSHIP OF A PRINCE OF WALES

Exposure to the media has not on the whole been a source of resentment to the Prince of Wales – even such cruel parries as a description of him as a "Royal borderliner" when it was announced that he would be going up to Cambridge have not been allowed to rancour – what it does represent, however, is a constant and relentless reminder of George III's warning to his own son, "The behaviour of royalty should be the examplar for the nation". In "humanizing" the Royal Family the media has in no way relieved its members of the sometimes onerous task of representing the best in humanity. Under modern scrutiny the historic duties of the heir to the throne are made, if anything, more apparent.

"If I'm deciding on whom I want to live with for the next fifty years," commented Prince Charles not so very long ago, "– well that's the last decision in which I'd want my head to be ruled entirely by my heart." A "humanized" image of the monarchy allows at least for the Prince to have a heart when it comes to a question which in earlier years was so frequently purely an instrument of political or financial expediency. Historical roots, however, still call for that heart to be governed with wisdom.

In April 1284, Queen Eleanor of Castile, consort of King Edward I of England, gave birth to a second male child at Caenarfon, the ancient centre of the Welsh princes of Gwynedd. Nearly seventeen years later, the boy, named Edward and by this time heir to the throne, was created "Prince of Wales" by his father at the Lincoln Parliament. So began an association of the royal heritage of Gwynedd with the English Crown which has survived to this day. So also began a tradition whereby most, although not all, of the eldest sons of English sovereigns have borne this title specifically granted by the reigning monarch.

Of the first twenty Princes of Wales, only seven were married while they bore the title and certainly few embarked on so serious an undertaking as matrimony for so trivial a reason as love. It is worth noting, however, that even when wife-hunting for the Prince of Wales was very much an instrument of State craft it was not without its devotees. Marriage negotiations excited gossip in the inns and taverns of London, long before the rise of the popular press and the omnipresent modern media made it a speculative sport for an intrigued populace at home and abroad. It did not, for example, escape commentators that when the Black Prince as Prince of Wales married Countess Joan of Kent in

October 1361 it was as much for money as for love or that he was the good lady's third husband!

The next Prince of Wales to marry before acceding to the Crown was Arthur, elder son of Henry VII. Born in 1486, he was invested as Prince of Wales at the age of four, by which time negotiations for his marriage to Catherine of Aragon had already been instigated by his father. The negotiations were a matter for statesmen and diplomats and the boy prince could hardly be expected to have much to say on the subject. In May 1499, after the marriage portion had been settled, Arthur was duly conducted to Bewdley for a proxy marriage ceremony in which he made his pledges to the bearded Spanish Ambassador. When in October he wrote to the woman to whom he was already married by proxy, the letter consisted understandably of a single page of stilted Latin compliments many of which doubtless owed their inspiration to the royal tutor.

Arthur's feelings on the subject of Catherine's arrival in England appear to have been determined almost entirely by the recommendations of his tutor, Sir Reginald Bray, and the King. For Henry VII it was of vital importance that his son should become a husband and, above all, a father – a son's son would secure the dynasty, still threatened by Yorkists with good claims to the succession. The fact too, that the new Princess of Wales was herself a distant claimant, was by no means insignificant.

Catherine's ship arrived in Plymouth on 2nd October 1501 but such was Arthur's enthusiasm that he did not even set out from Ludlow for the South until the end of the month. When he and his father did actually arrive within ten miles of where the Spanish princess was staying, her chaperones claimed that neither the bridegroom nor the King had the right to see her before the day of the wedding ceremony. The King, however, grew suspicious that the lady might be ugly and, in a brief concession to his son's sensibilities, insisted on meeting his future daughter-in-law. Arthur passively followed and watched on as his father and his younger brother danced with his bride-to-be.

The Royal Wedding was held in the old St Paul's Cathedral and was accompanied by days of pageantry in the streets. The Prince and Princess spent their first night together at the Bishop of London's Palace, close to St Paul's but their ill-fated marriage was to last only five months. Arthur's health gave way and in Easter week he died. The Prince of Wales' death was a source of personal distress to the King; it was also the cause of considerable political embarrassment for the Spanish wished to cement the alliance. Once again weighing sentiment, religious conscience

and diplomatic necessity, he turned to his younger son to safeguard the male succession in the Tudor dynasty and arranged yet another betrothal of convenience for Princess Catherine, this time to the future Henry VIII.

By the time George Augustus became the 14th Prince of Wales in 1714 he had already been married to Caroline of Anspach for eight years. Their son Frederick, however, sowed his wild oats as Prince of Wales for some time, setting the tongues of London wagging with tales of his amorous adventures. When he did demand marriage it was partly due to annoyance with his father for having arranged a marriage for the Princess Royal before showing any concern for his son's matrimonial interests, and partly due to financial incentives. Marriage would bring the Prince £50,000 a year from Wales instead of the £24,000 he received as a single man. When it came to the actual choice of a bride, the responsibility was not that of the Prince but of the King, who chose for political reasons a princess from one of the smaller Lutheran states.

Frederick's heir, Prince George William Frederick, did not marry until he had become George III but his method of selecting his Queen is worthy of note. Having been advised against marrying the lady who had won his heart, he simply succombed entirely to the dictates of his head and sat down with a copy of the "New Berlin Almanack for Princesses", finding an eminently suitable choice in Charlotte Sophia.

The saga of the dynastic marriage of their son, although formed on a similar basis, was considerably less successful. Born in August 1762 and created 17th Prince of Wales when he was only five days old, by the Spring of 1780 George Augustus Frederick was renowned for his romantic activities. Satirical cartoons of Perdita and her "Prince Florizel" on sale throughout London drew attention to one affair in particular. During a performance of Garrick's version of "The Winter's Tale", the Prince had fallen in love with the actress who played the part of Perdita and embarked upon a relationship in which he made rash promises of a wealthy future. One year later he had tired of the romance but was unable to extricate himself from the commitments he had made without a court case and a public scandal. "The Times" was relentless in its criticism, announcing to the world that the Prince of Wales was "like a hard-drinking, swearing man who at all times would prefer a girl and a bottle to politics and a sermon". The condemnation was somewhat unjust. The Prince of Wales was a shrewd connoisseur of the visual arts and possessed architectural imagination. It was he, for example, who

THE COURTSHIP OF A PRINCE OF WALES

transformed Brighthelmstone into Brighton. The London populace, however, were more concerned with salacious titbits about his private life and unfortunately, the Prince, far from learning his lesson, continued to cater to their appetite.

In March 1784, Maria Fitzherbert arrived in London for the season. The Prince of Wales once again fell hopelessly in love despite the fact that Mrs. Fitzherbert was a devout and virtuous Catholic who had no intention of becoming the latest in his succession of mistresses. His protestations of love were met with her expressed intention of going abroad but, after a series of dramatic episodes, they were married in secret by an Anglican curate. By the end of 1793, however, the Prince had again tired of a relationship which he knew could never be legally recognised under the Royal Marriage Act of 1772 or the Act of Settlement of 1701. With this in mind, he resolved to conclude a dynastic marriage with a Protestant bride, a course of action which he estimated was worth another £50,000 a year from Parliament.

Caroline of Brunswick, his own cousin, seemed in theory an expedient choice and without so much as meeting the lady, Prince George committed himself to marriage. Unfortunately when the two did meet he found his intended physically repulsive. Strangely, the marriage plans went ahead but the wedding three days later was something of a farce. The bride was constantly in danger of falling under the weight of her own dress and the bridegroom, we are told, was in a similar predicament because he was drunk.

Needless to say the marriage was a dismal failure and, sadly, the Prince was even denied the financial reward he had hoped for from Parliament. Inevitably he sought happiness and consolation in the arms of Mrs. Fitzherbert and so, at a time when he was already being attacked by cartoonists and condemned by newspapers for his extravagant life style, came the revelation of a matrimonial breakdown. As his father, George III, did not hesitate to point out to him, as an "exemplar for the nation" he had failed.

This, although with nowhere near the same degree of justification, was very much the attitude of Queen Victoria to her own son, Albert, when she received news that during his time at a military traning camp near Dublin, the Prince of Wales had entertained an actress in his rooms for the evening. A short time after the incident the Prince Consort collapsed and died, apparently from typhoid, but in the eyes of

Queen Victoria her eldest son, Bertie, who had been called upon to attain and maintain an almost impossible standard of conduct, was the cause of his father's illness and therefore responsible for his death. Nevertheless the "disgraceful affair" accentuated the need to find a bride for the 19th Prince of Wales, an idea which the Prince Consort had already proposed some time before Bertie had been dispatched for military training. Once again the "Almanack for Princesses" came in useful but this time it could be supplemented with photographs. There must be no risk of Bertie encountering difficulties similar to those suffered by his grandfather with Caroline of Brunswick. The Princess Royal recommended Alexandra, eldest daughter of Prince Christian of Denmark and Bertie was attracted to her photograph. A "chance encounter" was organised with meticulous care so that Bertie and Alexandra could "happen" to be sightseeing in Speyer Cathedral at the same time.

By the summer of 1862, Victoria, despite her own "unconquerable aversion to the Prince of Wales", evidently saw it as her duty to pursue arrangements for the young couple's marriage. Accordingly, the engagement was announced on 16th September and the eighteen-year-old princess arrived in England to be greeted with enthusiastic exuberance. Tennyson, the poet laureate of the day, spoke for the masses when he welcomed in verse the "sea king's daughter from over the sea", calling upon "all things youthful and sweet" to "scatter blossom under her feet". Despite a conspicuous degree of royal neglect of the Principality of Wales, the wedding of their titular prince aroused enthusiasm among the Welsh people. In August 1862 at the Caenarfon Eisteddfod it was resolved that the musician Brinley Richards and the poet Ceiriog Hughes should combine their respective talents to compile a princely anthem. By the end of the year Hughes had written "Ár Dywysog Gwlad y Bryniau" (On the Prince of Hills) which was then rather freely translated into English, set to Brinley Richards' music and played and sung during the marriage celebrations under the now familiar title, "God bless the Prince of Wales".

The wedding of Prince Albert Edward, subsequently King Edward VII, to Princess Alexandra was the last previous occasion on which the British public had the opportunity to celebrate the marriage of a Prince of Wales. The ceremony itself, however, was an essentially private affair, held in St George's Chapel, Windsor on 10th March 1863. The Queen approved of "dear Alex". Albert, she was convinced "would have loved her", and so there was only one possible place where

the marriage could be solemnised. In St George's Chapel a new east window, altar and reredos were being erected in memory of the Prince Consort. The Queen who, even on this joyful occasion had not cast-off her widow's weeds, watched from the Royal closet overlooking the altar, herself unseen by all but those immediately below. The Dean of Windsor, a personal friend who had knelt beside the death bed of the Prince Consort, had devised for her a private route from the Deanery over the leads of the Dean's Cloister to the Royal Closet. The service included a chorale composed by the Prince Consort and the ceremony, which should have been a source of joy to the Queen, was instead an event during which she "suffered indescribably". For the Prince it was the prelude to a marriage of good fortune for "sweet Alex" remained popular and treated with indulgence his succession of flirtations which the world at large branded as affairs and which earned him the title of "prince of pleasure".

George Frederick Albert, the second-born son of Edward VII and Alexandra was to marry Mary of Teck before he was created the nineteenth Prince of Wales. Their courtship and marriage were untroubled by the slightest suggestion of real scandal. The future George V's life was in fact so free from any food for gossip that towards the end of his principate someone actually took it upon himself to circulate a sensational tale of his own making. It was said that the Prince of Wales had embarked upon a secret marriage with the daughter of an Admiral while he was serving with the Mediterranean Fleet. This fabrication most likely began as a joke but it did find its way into a periodical and eventually had to be publically exposed as untrue. The misguided editor of the paper found himself dispatched to gaol for twelve months for criminal libel and the Prince of Wales emerged with the record of his private life unblemished. Later, as George V and Queen Mary, the royal couple were regarded as pillars of moral rectitude who, despite Queen Mary's greater flexibility and sympathy, undoubtedly together represented a rather stiff and forbidding front to their eldest son, the next Prince of Wales.

Prince Edward Albert Christian George Andrew Patrick David was created Prince of Wales in 1910 at the age of sixteen, and the summer of 1911 witnessed the revival of the ceremony of the public investiture at Caenarfon. The young Prince struck a handsome figure in his regalia and photographs of the occasion sold in their thousands throughout England and Wales. It was a summer of discontent, fraught with industrial problems and it was by this time inevitable that newspapers should attempt to raise the general tone of gloom by inciting speculation as to whom this Prince Charming would choose as his Princess. In the spring of 1911 Princess Victoria Louise, daughter of the Kaiser had accompanied her parents on a visit to England. During the unveiling of a memorial to Queen Victoria which the three foreign guests attended, the Princess committed the cardinal sin of actually being seen to stand next to the Prince of Wales. This insignificant event was enough to trigger off unbridled talk of a romance, despite the fact that the Princess was Prince Edward's senior by twenty-one months, considerably more mature and eventually married the Duke of Brunswick.

The Prince's private life during the twenties and thirties no doubt appeared flippant and irresponsible to the King and his older generation of advisers. Edward enjoyed a hectic social life. He was also the

first Prince of Wales to be photographed smoking a cigarette, to play polo, to fly a plane or to ride in point-to-point steeple chases. His distinctive voice was frequently heard on the wireless and the famous song, "I've danced with a man who's danced with a girl who's danced with the Prince of Wales", accurately reflects the adulation in which he was held by younger members of the public, particularly the female contingent.

The press treated their Prince's activities with the respect and restraint which the British public still expected of any dealings with members of the Royal Family. Nevertheless the bride-hunting continued. Society was by no means short of aspiring Cupids but of all those who tried their hand at match-making, surely the most incongruous figure must be that of Joachim von

Ribbentrop, the Nazi party adviser on foreign affairs, who tried to arrange a marriage between the Prince and the daughter of the Duke and Duchess of Brunswick, informing them that Herr Hitler would smile upon such a match. Needless to say, the Duchess, whose own name some years earlier had been linked with that of the Prince, refused to oblige Herr Hitler. Von Ribbentrop, did not, however, altogether

Above and left Prince Charles' visit to Mother Teresa's Sanctuary for Homeless Children in Calcutta, during his tour of India in December 1980. Opposite page, top His head respectfully covered, he enters the Jama Msjid Mosque, Delhi. Opposite page, below The Prince tours a bird sanctuary by boat as part of his 12-day visit.

abandon his interest in the Prince of Wales' affairs of the heart. During a mission to London in 1935 he made a point of inviting Mrs. Wallis Simpson to dinner at the German Embassy where the guest of honour was the Prince of Wales.

After the death of King George V, King Edward VIII reigned for only 326 days. Of this brief time, over a month was spent with Mrs. Simpson on a cruise in the Aegean and the Adriatic and a further period was passed with her on a visit to Vienna. The American and Continental press soon took up the story; the British press remained remarkably silent until some time after 16th November

THE TWENTY-FIRST PRINCE OF WALES

when Edward informed the then Prime Minister, Mr. Baldwin, that he intended to marry Mrs. Simpson as soon as her divorce from her second husband was made absolute, and that in order to do so he was prepared, if necessary, to abdicate. The question which was mulled over repeatedly at the Cabinet meetings of the closing months of 1936 was whether the British and Dominion Governments believed that their people would tolerate the sovereign's marriage to a woman who had already divorced two husbands. The conclusion was that despite a "Stand by the King" campaign (which in fact aroused little support for him), they would not. A marriage of this kind would be incompatible with the King's role as "Supreme Governor" of the Church of England, and a morganatic marriage which would deny the King's wife the status of Queen was not considered a satisfactory alternative.

The instrument of abdication was prepared and became effective on Friday, 11th December 1936. Prince Edward's speech explaining his decision to follow the dictates of his heart announced via the wireless to the Empire that he felt he would have been unable to "discharge my duties as King as I would wish to do without the help and support of the woman I love". The attitude of the British public had remained almost unanimously consistent throughout. Divorce and remarriage may well be tolerated in society at large but any lowering of standards in the monarchy was deplorable and unacceptable.

Even a cursory glance at the various Princes of Wales and their marriages reveals a precedent for most of the scale positions in the delicate balance between heart and head; and the question inevitably arises as to where such precedents leave Prince Charles, the 21st Prince of Wales, the man whom the media has portrayed as "the world's most eligible bachelor" and the man who had no hesitation in telling students in Winnipeg that his aim was to "change the old remote image of royalty".

"The Princess Elizabeth, Duchess of Edinburgh, was safely delivered of a Prince at 9.14pm. Her Royal Highness and her son are both doing well": this relatively simple notice on the railings at Buckingham Palace announced the birth of the first male in direct succession to the throne for more than eighty years. His ancestors included such unlikely figures as Mohammed, the Prophet of Islam, and George Washington, the first President of the United States, and he was born to bear a range of titles which are at the very least impressive. Prince Charles' formal title is His Royal Highness the Prince Charles

THE TWENTY-FIRST PRINCE OF WALES

Philip Arthur George, Prince of Wales and Earl of Chester, Duke of Cornwall and Rothesay, Earl of Carrick and Baron of Renfrew, Lord of the Isles and Great Steward of Scotland, Knight of the Garter. Above all, however, the child whose birth was announced on 14th November 1948 was born to be King. The fact did not really dawn on him until he was about eight years old when it did so "in the most ghastly, inexorable sense". It only gradually became apparent that, as Prince Charles himself has put it, "people are interested in you and you slowly get the idea that you have a certain duty and responsibility". From the very first, however, the Queen was determined to prepare her son for the task of one day representing an institution increasingly subject to attack and reigning over a kingdom which has known better days. Queen Elizabeth II shared with her mother the conviction that King George VI's death was accelerated by his untimely accession to the throne on the abdication of Edward VIII. Nothing in his life had prepared him for it and his famous stammered comment to his mother, Queen Mary, on learning that he must assume the role of King, "B-b-but, I cannot even speak properly, Mama", was a cry from the heart. Such an interruption of the smooth line of royal succession must never again occur. Prince Charles must be properly equipped for the monarchy. He must also be made to recognise at an early age the importance of his own childrens' role in securing the

dignity and the continuity of the Royal line. These objectives became the subject of careful planning. It is no accident for example, that Prince Andrew has for many years been tailored as principal understudy, capable if necessary of taking over at a moment's notice, or that no two members of the Royal Family next to each other in

THE TWENTY-FIRST PRINCE OF WALES

succession to the throne ever travel in the same aircraft. Prince Charles never flies with the Queen or with Prince Andrew.

Undoubtedly this kind of thinking was instilled into the Prince of Wales at an early age but if the Queen was determined to imbue her eldest son with a sense of royal responsibility, she was equally adamant that he should be allowed as normal a childhood as possible. As a boy, Charles was protected for the most part from the broad arena of ceremonial public life. Instead, unlike his predecesors, he was sent out into the world to meet his future subjects at a more personal level. The Queen had been educated within the confines of Buckingham Palace by a succession of private tutors. Charles, she felt,

This page and opposite *Prince Charles enjoys sailing and fishing while visiting Western Australia in March 1979.*

THE TWENTY-FIRST PRINCE OF WALES

should be given the opportunity to venture outside the royal stockade to rub up against other children. Her view was shared by Prince Philip: "We want him to go to school with other boys of his generation and to learn to live with other children. To absorb from his childhood the discipline imposed by education with other children." Prince Philip also wanted his son to be subjected to the rough and tumble of sporting activity with other youngsters. Accordingly, a rather shy and retiring Prince Charles was sent first as a pupil to Hill House, Knightsbridge and then to his father's old preparatory school, Cheam School in Berkshire. Again, as a result of his father's influence, when Charles reached public school age, he was dis-

patched, not to Eton, the traditional establishment for top young English gentlemen, but rather to Gordonstoun, a school in Scotland with a reputation for spartan discipline designed to build masculine character. Prince Philip felt that his time there had done him good and that a curriculum which included emptying dustbins, gardening, waiting at table and an early morning run followed by a cold shower, would be beneficial to his son. Charles, somewhat apprehensive at the prospect, was flown to Gordonstoun and duly instructed not to "let the side down". Despite his initial dislike of the school and in defiance of acute attacks of home-sickness, Charles did not "let the side down" and eventually grew to enjoy it as much as his father had done before him. He became an active sportsman, captaining the school's cricket and hockey teams and representing Gordonstoun at inter-school athletics meetings. He also played the

THE TWENTY-FIRST PRINCE OF WALES

Above *Prince Charles at polo.* Above right *Skiing at Klosters, in Switzerland.* Opposite page: Far Left *With labrador Harvey at Balmoral, 1978.* Top *A canter at Ascot.* Centre *Polo at Windsor in 1979.* Below *National Hunt rider.*

title role in a production of "Macbeth". After a year spent at Timbertops, an open-air school in the mountains of Australia – an interval which Prince Charles himself looked back on as "the most wonderful period" of his life because as the "Pommie Prince" he was so completely accepted – he returned to Gordonstoun to become head boy. He passed his "A" levels in History and French and in October 1967 went up to Trinity College, Cambridge, to read social anthropology and archaeology.

The Prince arrived at Trinity on the afternoon of October 8th, driving his own red Mini. He was welcomed at the Great Gate by Lord Butler, then Master of the College, and

escorted to his rooms on Staircase E of New Court, a small suite which the Queen had already inspected and found "plain but comfortable". Apart from the concessions which must be made to considerations of security and the steady increase in his commitment to a public role, the intention was that Prince Charles should lead, as far as possible, the life of any other undergraduate. College rules stipulated that the red Mini must be abandoned within Cambridge itself, and the vision of the Prince of Wales speeding through the city streets on a bicycle became a familiar sight which, much to Prince Charles' satisfaction, ceased to provoke comment in the local people. He joined university societies, particularly those devoted to amateur theatricals, appearing in the Trinity Revue "Revolution" to mock a cliché repeatedly used by less ardent royalists. Standing solemnly beneath an umbrella, he undoubtedly endeared himself to his audience by intoning plaintively, "I lead a sheltered life". For polo, his favourite

sport, he won his half-blue as the youngest member of the university team and as an accomplished cellist there was never any question of his neglecting his music. The more cynical had reservations as to whether the Prince would actually settle to the three years of academic work required for the Tripos but in the summer of 1968 he sat the first part and passed with a good Second Class Honours. He then transferred to the faculty of History and, despite the fact that his course was interrupted to spend a term at the University College of Wales at Aberystwyth, where he studied Welsh History, language and culture, he still managed to take his finals at Cambridge in May 1970 and obtain a Second Class Bachelor of Arts Degree.

Almost inevitably, by the time Prince Charles was twenty, royal functions were beginning to demand more and more of his time. In the summer of 1958 at the conclusion of the Commonwealth Games and while Charles was still a rather shy if mischievous

THE TWENTY-FIRST PRINCE OF WALES

schoolboy at Cheam, the Queen had created her son Prince of Wales and announced her intention of presenting him to the Welsh people at Caernarfon when he had grown up. The investiture at Caernarfon Castle was the most significant ceremonial event to mark the gradual increase in the Prince's public role. Most of Wales welcomed the investiture but extremist members of the Welsh nationalist party deplored the continuance of "Anglo-Norman" supremacy in their homeland. Thirteen bombs were exploded by nationalist fanatics in the months preceding the investiture. Yet, despite these protests, the occasion was a happy one. The Prince was able to respond to the loyal address in both English and Welsh, and the sincerity with which he committed himself to an identification with Wales was readily apparent: "It is my firm intention to associate myself in word and deed with as much of the life of the Principality as possible."

While he was still at Cambridge, Prince Charles, as Earl of Chester, took his seat in the House of Lords. During the years which followed his graduation, he tried with a remarkable degree of conscientiousness to divide his time between honouring his promise to the people of Wales, fulfilling his public engagements and gaining experience of life in the Royal Air Force and the Royal Navy. As a pilot in both Forces, Prince Charles has flown every type of aircraft from commando helicopters to Phantom jet fighters. His first parachute jump during his R.A.F. training nearly ended in disaster when he found himself falling with his legs caught in the rigging lines but he passed out from Cranwell, after completing the advanced flying course, in August 1971. Only two months later he was at Dartmouth as a Sub-Lieutenant, Royal Navy, and in the course of his naval training he was posted to a number of vessels, eventually to be given command of the minehunter H.M.S. Bronington. When he retired from such active involvement in the Royal Navy, it was due to the almost intolerable pressure of official duties yet with characteristic conscientiousness he believed it wrong that he should wear the uniform of a Colonel-in-Chief of the Parachute Regiment without himself being trained as a paratrooper. Despite his earlier mishap with a parachute, in order to wear his parachutist's wings with some degree of understanding, he insisted on undertaking the full paratroop officer's course.

In between his endless list of official engagements, ranging through every possible duty from the opening of a steelworks in Cardiff to the supervision of the Queen's Silver Jubilee Appeal, a campaign designed to "help young people help themselves", the

Above *Prince Charles' serious side.* Opposite *In New Zealand, in April.*

Prince of Wales has somehow found time to embark upon the kind of adventures that have made him the envy of every schoolboy. He has dived under the Artic ice, an experience reserved for only the most intrepid of the sub-aqua fraternity, he has hunted for Russian submarines as the captain of a warship, he has driven a team of Eskimo huskies on the frozen wastes of the Northwest Frontier, and more recently he has taken up the dangerous sport of steeplechasing. In all this he has been shadowed more relentlessly than any of his predecessors by the public eye. Photographers and journalists have pursued him, ever eager for an off-the-cuff remark or a fortuitous shot of him in the company of some pretty girl. Remarkably he has survived this unprecedented degree of exposure to achieve his own objective of changing the old remote image of royalty and to emerge under the generally complimentary guise of "action man" or "Prince Charming". At a time when the Queen and Prince Philip in their middle years no longer – as Prince Philip himself has pointed out – possessed quite the same shining appeal that they did in their youth, Prince Charles appeared to inject new life into the monarchy.

As a graduate, musician, actor, pilot, naval officer, parachutist, international polo-player, steeplechaser, jockey, public speaker, leader and royal ambassador, the Prince of Wales has won the respect of the world. His accomplishments coupled with a sense of humour, which he himself sees as his saving grace, have meant that he can be subjected to that most critical process of "humanization" without appearing any less worthy of his

role. "Were it not for my ability to see the funny side of my life, I'd have been committed to an institution long ago" – the admission betrays both honesty and that characteristic which never fails to appeal to the British people, the capacity to see oneself in a humorous light. Asked once by David Frost how he would describe himself, Prince Charles replied unhesitatingly: "Sometimes, a bit of a twit".

"The most important quality a person like myself needs", the Prince insists, "is a sense of humour and the ability to laugh at oneself". Humour takes the sting out of such criticism as has been levelled at him, very largely for such trivial offences as holding his hands behind his back like his father, a habit which he has attributed to the fact that they share the same tailor, or for being too conservative in his dress. The response somehow exposes the critic as unworthy: "I dare say that I could improve my image in some circles by growing my hair to a more fashionable length, being seen at the Playboy Club at frequent intervals, and squeezing myself into tight clothes"... "I was once asked whether I concentrated on developing my image – as if I was some kind of washing powder, presumably with a special blue whitener. I have absolutely no idea what my image is, therefore I intend to go on being myself to the best of my ability." That self has proved to be a remarkably competent one and the fact that the Prince has been able to be open about what "shortcomings" he does have, be it his natural shyness, or his ineptitude at mathematics, has served only to increase his popularity.

If the Prince of Wales' success is to be attributed in some measure to a masterplan designed to ensure the continuity of the monarchy by producing an heir to the throne capable of understanding and meeting the contemporary demands of a traditional role, then it would appear to have worked. Prince Charles' approach to his role is one coloured above all by a strong sense of responsibility: "I maintain that the greatest function of any monarchy is the human concern which its representatives have for the people especially in what is becoming an increasingly inhuman era – an age of computers, machines, multi-national organisations. This, to my mind is where the future can be promising." Of the modern monarchy he has said: "There isn't any power but there can be influence. The influence is in direct proportion to the respect people have for you," and his present role as Prince of Wales is one committed to the traditional motto, "Ich dien" or "I serve". "I believe it best to confine myself to three basic aims at the start, to show concern for people, to display an interest in them as individuals, and to

encourage them in a whole host of ways"…
"I serve" is a marvellous motto to have, and I think that it's the basis of one's job. If you have a sense of duty, and I like to think I have, then service is something that you give to people, particularly if they want you – but sometimes if they don't. If you feel that you can do something…then you can be of service."

The multitude of ways in which Prince Charles' desire to serve has manifested itself have not failed to catch the public eye. There has only been one issue on which the Prince has been relatively slow to come forward and that is the issue of marriage. Inevitably this fact also did not fail to catch the public eye. Like his great-uncle before him, the Prince of Wales had but to be seen in the presence of a pretty girl and the newspapers and magazines circulated hints of a prospective marriage. By the time he was in his mid-twenties Prince Charles, by his own admission, had been in love many times. "I've fallen in love with all sorts of girls and I fully intend to go on doing so," he announced defiantly. The public were sympathetic to the needs of the Prince to find a wife whom he could promise to love for the rest of his life. A Prince now manifestly endowed with feelings "just like anybody else" could no longer be expected to take recourse to that much-thumbed "Almanack of Princesses", and the image of the "world's most eligible bachelor" enjoying the company of a succession of the world's beautiful women and delighting in being on the receiving end of the popular pastime of kissing the Prince of Wales, was not without its rugged masculine appeal. By the time, however, the Prince at thirty-one was still a bachelor, there were those who felt that the long list of romances, both fictitious and real, was beginning to verge on the ridiculous. There is some suggestion that the Queen, all too acutely aware that the image of monarchy is no more than the combined images of those who represent it, was concerned that the Prince's image, in love at least, was becoming that of the Playboy. "Charlie's Darlings" were gaining the same kind of attention as "Prince Florizel's" had before them. Prince Philip, ever the realist, did not mince words in advising his son: "It's about time you got on with it. If you wait much longer, there won't be any suitable girls left – and you'll be on the shelf, my boy." The unvoiced criticism that the Prince of Wales' delay in choosing a wife bordered on the irresponsible was implicit in all kinds of quarters.

Prince Charles' whole approach to the question of marriage, however, belied all suggestion of irresponsibility. It spoke rather of that strong sense of royal duty which had

Opposite *At Rio de Janiero in 1978, Prince Charles enjoys an exotic and energetic night out.* Above *Lieutenant the Prince of Wales commands the minesweeper HMS Bronington during a naval exercise involving his squadron in the Firth of Forth in November 1976.* Right *The Prince relaxes in his cabin after the exercise.* Below *Prince Charles with Prince Andrew at a polo match at Windsor Great Park in 1980: Prince Andrew has not followed his elder brother's active and consuming love of equestrian sports.*

THE LADY DIANA SPENCER

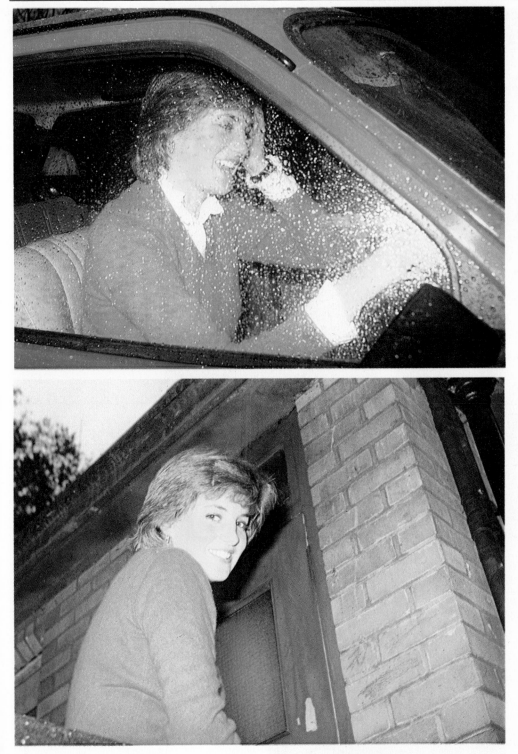

be king. I've received a special education and training. I could never be a normal person because I've been prepared to reign over my subjects." For one with so strong a sense of duty there could be no question of abdication for love. In choosing a wife, he was aware that he might well be choosing a future queen: "You have to remember that when you marry in my position, you're going to marry someone who, perhaps, is one day going to be queen. You've got to choose somebody very carefully, I think, who could fulfil this particular role, and it has got to be somebody pretty unusual." "Marriage", he insisted, "is a much more important business than falling in love, essentially a question of mutual love and respect for each other. Creating a secure family unit in which to bring up children, to give them a happy, secure upbringing – that's what marriage is all about, creating a home." For him marriage, he knew, must be for life: "I have a particular responsibility to ensure that I make the right decision. The last thing I could possibly entertain is getting divorced." His conclusion was all too readily comprehensible: "To me, marriage – which may be for fifty years – seems to be one of the biggest and most responsible steps to be taken in one's life. Which makes it all so hideously complicated!"

To add to this complexity, in a hereditary monarchy the requirements and the lessons of history are inescapable. The Royal Marriages Act of 1772, "An act for better regulating the future marriages of the Royal Family" instigated by George III, still provides that any descendants of George II, both male and female, are required to obtain the consent of the Sovereign before any marriage is contracted. Prince Charles' choice of wife must meet with the Queen's approval and, under the Act of Settlement of 1701, his bride must not be a Roman Catholic. There have been several occasions when the Queen has considered pressing for this latter Act to be repealed, but it remained an obstruction when Prince Michael of Kent wished to marry the Austrian-born Baroness Marie-Christine von Reibnitz, whose previous marriage had been annulled. The marriage was permitted but Prince Michael was compelled to renounce his right of succession to the throne.

Historic precedents and parallels are never very far away. The current relevance of the headlines which greeted the announcement of the engagement of Princess Elizabeth and Lieutenant Philip Mountbatten, "Plans for Royal Wedding bring temporary relief to atmosphere of depression", cannot fail to strike a chord of recognition. To Prince Charles whose profound interest in history extends much further than the wedding of

Opposite The pictures that earned her the title *"Shy Di". Throughout Summer and Autumn, 1980, Lady Diana never once broke under constant pressure from newsmen who followed her from her flat to the kindergarten where she worked.* Top *She takes it all in good part as she drives away.* Above *A good-humoured smile as she arrives at the kindergarten.* Right *The building in Kensington where she shared a flat.*

been instilled into him from birth: "I'm not a normal person in the sense that I was born to

THE LADY DIANA SPENCER

his parents, the message "marry for love, but marry sensibly" must have proclaimed itself vociferously from every ancestral portrait.

Historians looking back upon Prince Charles' search for a bride will no doubt reflect with all the unquestionable wisdom of hindsight that Lady Diana Spencer was a perfectly obvious and ideal choice from the start. Since his engagement the Prince of Wales has made a humourous reference to the fact that he has at last been able to give up wandering hopefully around with a glass slipper. Fairy-tale and romance would have made the possible future Queen of England a Cinderella. In reality it is far more expedient that she should belong to one of England's oldest and most aristocratic families. "The real aristocracy in this country is that which existed before the Industrial Revolution when lots of people who owned factories were given titles" – Harold Brooks-Baker, Managing Director of Debrett's Peerage, the

THE LADY DIANA SPENCER

Opposite, top *Lady Diana in September 1980.* Opposite, below *With kindergarten charges that September.* Above and right *Schoolboy·chivalry at Cheltenham, March 1981.*

arbiter of lineage in England is most emphatic: "There are only about 150 families that fall into this category." Lady Diana's father, the eighth Earl of Spencer heads such a lineage. The Earl's ancestry is full of Royal connections. The family tree links him to more than one king and Lady Diana and Prince Charles, it transpires, are sixteenth cousins once removed. The Spencer family motto "God defend the Right" originated in the sixteenth century when Warwickshire-born John Spencer, who made a fortune from sheep farming, was knighted by Henry VIII. The first Lord Spencer was made a baron in 1603 and eventually became one of the wealthiest men in England. His grandson was created the first Earl of Sunderland by Charles I and the second Earl became adviser to a succession of

three monarchs: Charles II, James II and William III. One branch of the family subsequently went on to become Dukes of Marlborough; the other branch became the Spencers. From the point of view of lineage Lady Diana's qualifications are impeccable and as if those qualifications required reinforcement her family's actual association with Royalty is equally strong.

Lady Diana's grandmother is a lady-in-waiting to the Queen Mother. Her father was equerry to George VI until the King's death and subsequently to his daughter, the Queen, who together with Prince Philip was among the 1,700 guests invited to the marriage of the then Viscount Althorp to Frances Ruth Burke Roche, daughter of the fourth Baron Fermoy in 1954. Lady Sarah, the first-born daughter of Viscount and Viscountess Althorp, was born in 1955. It was her name which was associated with that of Prince Charles for some time but Lady Sarah in fact married ex-Coldstream Guards officer and Old Harrovian Neil McCorquedale in May 1980. The middle daughter, Lady Jane, was born in 1957 and she, in her turn, was to

THE LADY DIANA SPENCER

hood there was spent in close proximity to the children of the Royal Family who, it is said, spent hot summers' afternoons in the Althorp's heated swimming pool. It was Prince Andrew, however, who was Lady Diana's regular playmate and not Prince Charles, who as a young man thirteen years her senior, was sent away to school while she was still a toddler. Her first governess, Gertrude Allen, remembers that toddler as a happy but conscientious child and Lady Diana, herself, recalls the days at Park House as "a good time of my life".

Sadly, the marriage between Edward John Spencer and Frances Fermoy, which had begun so splendidly as "Wedding of the Year" in the magnificent aisles of Westminster Abbey, did not last. At the age of thirty-one Frances decided she must build a new life for herself. The servants reported quite simply that she "just was not there any

A day for celebration: Prince Charles and his bride-to-be at Buckingham Palace on 24th February shortly after announcing their engagement.

make a "good marriage" – to Robin Fellowes, the son of the Queen's agent at Sandringham, at one time Prince Charles' private secretary and now the Queen's assistant private secretary.

The choice of godparents over the years has forged an even closer link between the Spencers and the Royal Family. Queen Mary and the late Duke of Windsor were godparents to the present Earl and the Queen is godmother to Lady Diana's younger brother Charles, the present heir to the earldom.

Lady Diana was born at Sandringham on 1st July 1961 and was christened there by a former Bishop of Norwich. Her parents at that time occupied Park House on the edge of the Sandringham Estate and her child-

more" and the Viscountess Spencer became the focal point of a scandal. She was named as the co-respondent in the divorce of wallpaper millionaire Peter Shand Kydd and his wife, Janet, and branded the "other woman" with all the condemnatory overtones that the sixties could provide. There was acrimonious argument over the custody of the children, which was eventually awarded to the Viscount and in the very same year Frances married Peter Shand Kydd. The divorce and remarriage meant that the

THE LADY DIANA SPENCER

children saw little of their mother and it was perhaps fortunate that, during much of this difficult time, Lady Diana was a pupil at Riddlesworth Hall, a preparatory school housed in a rambling mansion, at Diss in Norfolk. Riddlesworth has an excellent reputation for academic results but it is not for her academic achievements that Lady Diana is remembered there. Active by nature, she was good at sports, especially swimming and in those early years before a fall which was to cause her to lose her nerve, she loved horse-riding. Above all, however, she was "sweet with the little ones".

In 1975, when Diana was fourteen, Edward Spencer inherited the family seat from his father, Jack. As the eighth Earl, he left the ten-bedroomed Park House for the magnificent 16th century ancestral home, Althorp House, in Northamptonshire. Althorp, pronounced with traditional

later when the Earl decided to marry Raine, then Countess of Dartmouth, and daughter of the best-selling romantic novelist, Barbara Cartland.

Lady Diana was by this time a pupil at West Heath, a boarding school in Sevenoaks, Kent, where Queen Mary, wife and consort of George V was educated. West Heath aims to provide a sound general education and to encourage its pupils both to "develop their own minds and tastes" and to "realise their duties as citizens". Lady Diana's tastes proved to lie in the direction of art, classical music, ballet and history. Academically, her reports suggest a "normal and average" ability but she had a natural artistic talent and excelled at dancing. Amongst her fellow pupils she was renowned for being cheerful, fun-loving and considerate and those who shared her dormitory also delight in pointing out a fact now inevitably imbued with a

First official function: stunningly dressed, Lady Diana accompanies Prince Charles to a charity gala in London on 9th March. Right *With Princess Grace of Monaco in the foyer.*

English idiosyncracy "Altrup", has been the family seat of the Spencers for 473 years. Standing in a 15,000 acre estate, it contains the cream of the contents of five homes once owned by the Spencer family and one of the finest art collections in Britain, if not the world. The transition to a house ornamented with the works of Rubens, Poussin, Van Dyke, Gainsborough and Reynolds must have required a certain amount of adjustment on the part of the Spencer family. Re-adjustment was required only a short time

THE LADY DIANA SPENCER

touch of romantic symbolism. For some considerable time Diana slept beneath a photograph presented to the school by former newspaper head, Cecil King and depicting the Prince of Wales at his investiture.

Lady Diana did not take "A" levels and at sixteen, felt ready to leave school. Her father, however, felt equally strongly that she should continue her education. The result was a compromise. Lady Diana was sent to the exclusive Insitut Alpin Videmanette, a finishing school in Rougemont, Switzerland, where the quite intensive curriculum is designed to ensure that the young ladies are "healthy and happy" by helping them to "work hard and play hard in a relaxed family atmosphere". During her brief stay at the Institut Lady Diana took domestic science and learned the art of dressmaking and cooking. She also perfected her French and became an accomplished skier. Relaxation was as carefully controlled as work. There was little time to escape to the nearby resort of Gstaad and outings were generally conducted under the solicitous eye of a chaperone.

Lady Diana did not complete the course in Switzerland. Suffering from a severe bout of homesickness she returned to England for the Easter holidays and did not go back for the summer term. Instead she returned briefly to Althorp Hall. Near-tragedy had brought the Spencer children closer to their step-mother who in the first instance had not been particularly well received into the family. The Earl, under considerable pressure to ensure the smooth-running of Althorp, had collapsed in the stable yard with a massive brain haemorrhage, and it was largely due to his second wife's relentless efforts on his behalf that his health was restored. Only a slight blurring of his voice and a degree of hestitation in his speech now remain as a vestige of his long coma. At the time Lady Diana returned from Switzerland, however, her father was still in need of quiet and constant attention. There was little she could add to the help and concern which was already surrounding him and so it was decided that she should have a home of her own in London. The Earl bought her a generously proportioned three-bedroomed flat at Coleherne Court in Old Brompton Road, South Kensington where, in the company of three friends – Virginia Pitman, a Cordon Bleu cookery student, Carolyn Pride, a music student and Anne Bolton, she was able to lead something of a bachelor-girl existence.

Left *A serene Lady Diana at Goldsmith's Hall.* Opposite *Prince Charles welcomed at Wellington, New Zealand, by Robert Muldoon on 31st March.*

HISTORY'S MOST PUBLIC WOOING

In previous years, parents of aristocratic British families have not been renowned for their concern about whether or not their daughters had a particular profession or career in mind. Until relatively recently such parents were more concerned that their off-spring should "come out" in a London season of cocktail parties and grand balls. The ultimate goal was a "suitable" marriage.

Humour on duty: Prince Charles and his fiancée plant a commemorative tree at Broadlands, the home of the late Earl Mountbatten, with Lord and Lady Romsey. Far left and below Lady Diana meets the people.

with undisguised affection. Those who know Lady Diana never fail to comment on her love for children. Her temperament, they claim, is ideally suited to coping with small children. A calm firmness frequently followed by a smile and the now famous giggle is highly effective in winning their regard. Working at the kindergarten was the one part of her life that she admitted she would miss after the announcement of her engagement.

More recently, however, the traditional ceremony of "coming out" has declined in popularity – the Queen has never really liked the idea – and Lady Diana, like her sisters before her, shunned the debutante set, choosing instead to take a job. At the "Young England Kindergarten", run by two of Lady Diana's old school-friends, she worked with fifty toddlers who remember "Miss Diana"

Despite the fact that their early years were spent in such close proximity to one another, neither Prince Charles nor Lady Diana really remember meeting until November 1977 when Lady Sarah Spencer introduced the Prince to her younger sister in the middle of a ploughed field. Prince Charles recalls "a splendid sixteen-year-old". "I remember thinking what fun she was then," he has since admitted. Doubtless there were other subsequent casual meetings, and meetings which were perhaps not so easily attributable to chance. In July 1980 Lady Diana joined

HISTORY'S MOST PUBLIC WOOING

Prince Charles and the Royal Family on the Royal Yacht Britannia for their annual visit to the Isle of Wight for Cowes week. Thanks to diversionary tactics, of which the Royal Family are past masters, Lady Diana was never spotted in Cowes Harbour. As far as the eyes of the world were concerned one of history's most public wooings did not really begin until Friday, 5th September 1980, when Lady Diana left London to join the Prince, the Queen and other members of the Royal Family for a weekend at Balmoral. This was by no means the first time that she had spent the weekend at the Royal Family's Scottish home but this, according to Prince Charles, was when they both began to "realise there was something in it". Publicly it was marked by an exclusive picture of the Prince fishing in the River Dee for salmon, watched by a virtually unidentifiable Lady Diana, privately it was recorded with a bouquet of red roses delivered to the flat in Old Brompton Road together with a handwritten note from the Prince of Wales.

Above left *Lady Diana enjoys childrens' company at Broadlands.* Left *The couple after their visit.* Above *Highgrove House, their future home.* Top and opposite *Visiting Tetbury in May.*

41

HISTORY'S MOST PUBLIC WOOING

This page and opposite *Scenes at Horse Guards Parade as Prince Charles takes the salute at the Trooping the Colour rehearsal in June.*

Another visit to Scotland followed. This time, however, in order to avoid attracting undue attention, Lady Diana stayed at Birkhall, the home of that most popular of all potential match-makers, the Queen Mother. Careful planning guaranteed privacy for a weekend but it could not distract public attention indefinitely. By the 18th September

HISTORY'S MOST PUBLIC WOOING

HISTORY'S MOST PUBLIC WOOING

Opposite and left *The Queen betrays tension following the shooting incident before the 1981 Trooping the Colour ceremony.* Above *Prince Charles with Prince Philip.* Top *Lady Diana's first balcony appearance, with Prince Charles and his family after the parade.*

camera men were waiting outside the kindergarten in Pimlico in full force. With characteristic consideration and in an attempt to avoid any further disruption to the children's routine, "Miss Diana" agreed to reward their patience by posing for pictures in the small park next to the nursery school. The result was a series of pictures which Fleet Street pronounced sensational but which proved a source of shy embarrassment to the lady. The sunlight shining through her skirt made it virtually transparent. "I was so nervous about the whole thing I never thought I'd be standing with the light behind me," she commented, betraying a degree of naiveté which has served only to enhance her popularity, and adding a remark which must go down in the annals of history: "I don't want to be remembered for not having a petticoat."

There is little doubt that during the months of July and August the Prince had spent many solitary hours in his personal apartments in Buckingham Palace. It is equally certain that the issue of marriage had been the subject of some considerable thought. Prince Charles had suddenly developed an interest in house-hunting. Buckingham Palace had issued an instruction to the management of the Duchy of Cornwall, which is responsible for the thousands of acres in Gloucestershire, Wiltshire and Devon owned by the Prince as part

HISTORY'S MOST PUBLIC WOOING

of his birthright, to look for a suitable large country home fit for the heir to the throne. In a tiny village of Doughton, near the market town of Tetbury, Prince Charles spotted the Highgrove Estate. He wandered over its 346 acres of farmland and the distinguished Georgian House set in their midst and resolved almost immediately that the four reception rooms, nine bedrooms, six bathrooms, and a fully self-contained nursery wing, would make an ideal home. Highgrove became Royal property for the princely sum of £800,000 but not before Lady Diana had been asked to give her female opinion on the subject. By comparison with Althorp, Highgrove was small, intimate and homely and Lady Diana is said to have pronounced it "perfect".

Throughout the autumn and following winter Prince Charles and Lady Diana returned repeatedly to Highgrove, arriving

and leaving in separate cars – long, late night or early morning drives and false trails designed to throw off the watching press marked these and any other meetings. By this time a picture of Lady Diana performing even so insignificant an action as getting into her red Mini Metro would receive "front page treatment" and in October she delighted the world by backing the Prince when he rode his horse, Allibar in an amateur riders' steeplechase at Ludlow Races. As the Prince concluded the race in second place, Lady Diana danced with excitement in the grandstand. Nevertheless, the couple left the racecourse in separate cars before going on to spend the weekend together at the home of a mutual friend.

Shortly afterwards the Queen's reported comment on Lady Diana, "She is a delightful girl. Charles could not find a more perfect partner", appeared to confirm that she would give her blessing to their marriage and to suggest that the interest which was now being shown throughout the world was justified. As Prince Charles' thirty-second birthday approached many anticipated that it would be accompanied by "an announcement about his future". Lady Diana was smuggled into Sandringham for the Prince of Wales' birthday party but the birthday

came and went without an engagement announcement and was followed by a period of separation alleviated only by conversations held via a crackling telephone wire to India. The Prince had embarked upon a three week Royal tour of the Indian sub-continent, originally planned to be undertaken in the company of Lord Mountbatten.

Prince Charles' absence represented a particularly trying interval for Lady Diana. The more ruthless foreign press were now bringing havoc to the kindergarten and

Above, above left and opposite Prince Charles, Lady Diana, Princess Margaret and the Queen Mother outside St Margaret's Church, Westminster after the wedding of Nicholas Soames and Catherine Weatherall. Top and far left Prince Charles with the bride and groom.

pursuing her wherever she went. The distinctive Mini Metro was duly moved and parked in odd places at unusual times and her flatmates acted as decoys. A police patrol appeared outside her flat but still the pressure from the media remained considerable. In particular an allegation that Lady Diana and Prince Charles had spent several hours together, for two nights in succession, in a carriage of the Royal train must have been highly distressing to two people who had been so careful to ensure that history would record a perfect courtship. Both Prince Charles and the Queen were furious. An unprecedented move by the Palace demanding a retraction demonstrated the

HISTORY'S MOST PUBLIC WOOING

high regard in which Lady Diana was held, for innuendos concerning the Prince's earlier relationships had met only with silent disregard. Lady Diana in her turn issued a denial, insisting that she had been at home in the company of her flatmates on the nights in question, and the world was inclined to believe her. Her behaviour throughout had been exemplary. She had shown considerable courage in dealing with the media, she had not once resorted to rudeness and her only comment in response to questions concerning the Prince had been a blush. If the protective arms of Buckingham Palace were beginning to envelop her it was because she had shown herself worthy of becoming England's future Queen.

Even when the world at large had more or less settled the question of the Prince of Wales' future wife, Prince Charles still displayed a reluctance to be rushed. By the time he returned from India, however, he had begun to make discreet inquiries as to how his marriage to Lady Diana would be received. The difference in their ages, he discovered, far from being a liability, was considered an advantage for gynaecological reasons. Suffice it to say that for the Prince of Wales to take a wife and subsequently find that she was unable to ensure the succession would be the kind of mistake that a Royal Family so acutely aware of the need to guarantee its future would never make. By Christmas the question of marriage must have been put to Lady Diana, at least hypothetically, for the Heads of the Commonwealth were informed that there was a possibility of a Royal Wedding during the following summer.

Christmas separated Prince Charles and Lady Diana once again. Lady Diana, suffering from an attack of flu, spent Christmas with her father at Althorp. Yet, despite her absence, the traditional celebration of the New Year at Sandringham was so beset by clicking photographers that the usually good relations between the press and the Royal Family were sadly marred. Prince Charles wished one group of pressmen "a very happy New Year" but could not resist adding: "but I hope your editors have a particularly nasty one." Such was the pressure of interest that the prospect of a skiing holiday which the Prince and Lady Diana had planned to spend together in the Swiss Alps had to be abandoned. On 23rd January Prince Charles flew to Zurich alone.

Two days after his return from Switzerland the world's most eligible bachelor finally committed himself. Over a candlelit dinner in his three-roomed bachelor apartments overlooking the Mall, he proposed to Lady Diana Spencer and she, to his professed surprise and delight, agreed

without hesitation to "take him on". The timing of the proposal had been carefully planned. Lady Diana, who over the years had developed a particularly close relationship with her mother, was due to leave England with the Shand Kydds for a holiday in Australia. In truly Royal tradition, the Prince had wanted her to have this time away from England to consider whether "it was all going to be too awful". The acceptance, however, was instantaneous.

Prince Charles, by his own admission, is an incurable romantic. He had said goodbye to his bachelor days in traditional style and plans for the impending marriage were to be conducted in a similar manner. The Queen and Prince Philip were the first to be informed. A phone call from the Prince to Earl Spencer followed very shortly. In a

HISTORY'S MOST PUBLIC WOOING

Left and right *Lady Diana accompanies Prince Charles at her first State banquet, given by King Khalid of Saudi Arabia at Claridge's in June.* Above *The couple with the royal party as the Queen converses with King Khalid.* Opposite *The Queen and Queen Mother arrive at Claridge's.* Overleaf *Happy informality brilliantly caught in these superb photographs of Prince Charles and his fiancée.*

---

gesture which touched and delighted the Earl, the Prince of Wales formally asked for his consent to the marriage. "I wonder", the Earl mused later, "what the Prince would have said if I had told him 'no'". The question was one which greatly amused the Prince's future father-in-law.

The engagement was to remain a closely guarded secret for some weeks yet. Lady Diana's return to England was carefully arranged to coincide with Prince Andrew's twenty-first birthday, a day on which the attention of the public would be focussing on Prince Charles' younger brother. The reunion took place at Highgrove only to be followed by a tragic incident which may have accelerated the decision to make the impending marriage public knowledge. Watched by Lady Diana, the Prince took his favourite horse, Allibar, for a gallop across the Downs at Lambourn. The Prince had just completed the seven miles when Allibar collapsed beneath him and died. Prince Charles was heartbroken, Lady Diana was in tears but still the couple were compelled to leave in convoy. Prince Charles' car was followed by a vehicle containing his fiancée who in turn was followed by a police escort. The episode may have accentuated the stress attached to the constant need for subterfuge. Whatever the thinking behind it, however, the official announcement came only a few days later on Tuesday, 24th February. Some time prior to it, the Prime Minister, Mrs.

HISTORY'S MOST PUBLIC WOOING

Above *Lady Diana arrives at Ascot with Prince Charles; 16th June.* Left *With Princess Alexandra; 17th June.* Opposite *With escort; 18th June.*

Thatcher, and other top cabinet ministers were informed. So too, was the Archbishop of Canterbury, Dr. Robert Runcie. On the Monday, Lady Diana joined Prince Charles, the Queen and Prince Philip for dinner at Buckingham Palace, and spent the night at Clarence House, the home of the Queen Mother, in a room which was to remain her refuge for the next few months.

At precisely eleven a.m. on 24th February the Buckingham Palace Press Office released a very simple message to the world: "It is with the greatest pleasure that the Queen and the Duke of Edinburgh announce the betrothal of their beloved son, the Prince of Wales, to the Lady Diana Spencer, daughter of the Earl Spencer and the Honourable Mrs. Shand Kydd."

In the Palace ballroom the Queen's pleasure was all too apparent, as the Lord Chamberlain interrupted an investiture: "Her Majesty has asked me to let you know that an announcement is being made at this moment in the following terms..." he went on to read the official announcement.

HISTORY'S MOST PUBLIC WOOING

Left and right *At Wimbledon Lady Diana stands to applaud the winner of the ladies' singles match.* Below *The instigator of a new fashion arrives for the première of the James Bond film, "For Your Eyes Only", and* bottom *she attends an exhibition at the Royal Academy.*

Outside the Palace the Band of the Coldstream Guards struck up with the tune, "Congratulations". In the House of Commons, Members of Parliament cheered enthusiastically as Mrs. Thatcher referred to the "great pleasure" the news had brought to the nation. The Archbishop of Canterbury announced the engagement during a General Synod debate on the highly appropriate subject of marriage, and in the small village of Doughton in which Highgrove, the Royal couple's future home stands, the occasion was marked by the placing of a red carpet in the one and only telephone box.

THE CHARLES AND DIANA INDUSTRY

It goes almost without saying that the interval following the announcement of a forthcoming Royal Wedding has been marked, above all, by an unprecedented degree of media coverage, finding its outlet in every conceivable form, from glossy magazines to video tapes. An hour-long video programme entitled "The Story of Prince Charles and Lady Diana" and including "fresh and exclusive sequences concerning the childhood and later school years of Lady Diana" was advertised as providing such intimate disclosures as how, as a pupil at Riddlesworth School "she won the cup in Pets Corner because of the kindly way she looked after her guinea pig". British television networks have set up special departments to cope exclusively with "Royal Wedding Features" and television organisations throughout the world have been queuing up to take live coverage of the wedding from the BBC and ITV. By April in excess of thirteen countries outside Europe had already booked satellite time with British Telecom and with all of Europe receiving pictures via the European Broadcasting Union links, the comment from British Telecom itself had to be: "it looks as if we shall be catering for the largest audience in the history of British television". The Royal Wedding must mean revenue for British Telecom and an opportunity to display to the world a happy event surrounded by pageantry and ceremonial carried out to perfection – a constructive role for the media which, it must be hoped, will cause such saddening reports as the alleged tapping of phone calls from Prince Charles to Lady Diana and the Queen, to pale into insignificance. If the glint in George Orwell's all-seeing eye, universal surveillance by electronic means, is drawing in, then its focussing for a while on a joyous and public occasion must be to the good.

It would be impossible to enumerate all those who stand to benefit from the interest shown in the Royal Wedding, both at home and abroad. The almost desperate rush in the souvenir trade must, however, form yet another all too obvious mark of the times. There is nothing new about the production of royal souvenirs. With the exception, strangely enough, of the birth of a royal baby, practically every other milestone in royal history – such as a coronation or a wedding – is used as an excuse by manufacturers to flood the market with keepsakes. When Edward VIII visited America for the first time as Prince of Wales he paused for a moment to sign a visitors' book, little dreaming that the picture taken of him at the time would subsequently be used to adorn thousands of keepsakes, from cigarette boxes to buttons.

The Royal School of Needlework's tribute to the Royal Wedding takes the form of a kneeler above *as featured in the Sunday Telegraph and a sampler* opposite *as featured in the Daily Telegraph.*

There has been something frenzied, however, about the response to the opportunity to produce Royal Wedding mementos in all shapes and sizes that speaks eloquently of a perhaps unprecedented need to boost production and sales. At a dinner marking the 125th anniversary of Auckland's Chamber of Commerce, Prince Charles commented on the fact that several manufacturers had had a field day since the announcement of his engagement. Some, he said, had even written to him before the announcement to ask why he had not yet become engaged. Others had jumped the gun in other respects: "Several manufacturers", I am told, "had designed medallions to coincide with the wedding with Westminster Abbey on the back."

An indication of the volume of investment in the souvenir business lies in the fact that it has taken out record insurance cover against the wedding's cancellation, postponement or any change of venue. So much memorabilia from the most exquisite jewelry to the ordinary ashtray has been committed to recording the date and venue that even a postponement could damage sales prospects in a way that Britain's "Wedding Industry" could ill afford. History shows that their concern is not altogether unfounded. A precedent was provided by the postponement of the Coronation of Edward VII who was compelled to undergo an appendix operation only one week before the official date of the ceremony. Accordingly the more cautious have simply marked their product 1981, avoiding the use of the actual date.

Caution is not, however, an epithet to be generally applied to the avalanche of souvenirs which range from beer mats and coin watches to "revived 45s" entitled "Diana" and tin badges marked with the warning, "Don't do it, Di". Barbara Cartland, the novelist and mother of the bride's stepmother, has not missed the opportunity to produce her collection of "Romantic Royal Marriages" and, in a bid to raise funds for the handicapped in this year of the disabled, tradition has quite understandably been thrown to the winds and an "official souvenir" produced. It is perhaps not unfair to suggest that anything and everything that could be turned into a souvenir has been. The cartoonist who depicted the Royal Wedding souvenir seller with a stall full of unembellished china, explaining to a potential customer that "Prince Charles has fallen off the mug" was not so very far from the truth.

Amidst all this, there is something reassuring about the appearance of commemorative items which traditionally mark royal events. The two British commemorative Wedding stamps, for example, are the latest in a succession of special stamps commemorating royal events. The first such issue was in

THE CHARLES AND DIANA INDUSTRY

SEYCHELLES
Royal Wedding
1981

OFFICIAL FIRST DAY COVER

Elizabeth the Queen Mother. The commemorative stamp for the Queen Mother's birthday featured a well-known portrait of Her Majesty by Norman Parkinson and was issued as "a special birthday present to the Queen Mother".

The stamps which mark the Wedding of Prince Charles and Lady Diana feature a portrait of the happy couple taken by the Prince's uncle, the Earl of Snowdon. They also provide an explanation as to why Prince Charles, who at 5ft 11ins is one inch taller than Lady Diana, appears through the lens of Lord Snowdon a good head above his bride. The Prince, it would seem, was made to stand on a wooden box in order to ensure that there was sufficient room above Lady Diana's head for the stamps to bear the Queen's head and the price. The pictures were approved by the Queen, Prince Charles and Lady Diana who were so impressed with them that similar photographs were used for the official Royal Wedding souvenir brochure.

Over seventy countries round the world will be issuing special stamps to celebrate the Royal Wedding. A number of Commonwealth countries in particular, (Ascension Island, Barbados, Bermuda, the British Virgin Islands, Brunei, the Cayman Islands,

Stamps from over seventy countries throughout the world feature Prince Charles and Lady Diana in a variety of poses and settings.

1935 to mark the Silver Jubilee of the accession of King George V. This was followed by the Coronation stamp of May 1937 and in 1948 by two stamps marking the Silver Wedding anniversary of George VI and Queen Elizabeth (now the Queen Mother). Since then British stamps have paid tribute to the investiture of the Prince of Wales, the Silver Wedding anniversary of the Queen and the Duke of Edinburgh, the Wedding of Princess Anne and Captain Mark Phillips, the Queen's Silver Jubilee and the eightieth birthday of Her Majesty Queen

the Falkland Islands, Fiji, The Gambia, Hong Kong, Lesotho, Mauritius, Norfolk Islands, Pitcairn Islands, St. Helena, Somoa, Sierre Leone, The Soloman Islands, Swaziland, Tristan da Cunha and Vanuatu) have chosen to affirm their loyalty and affection by issuing special postage stamps with the result that the Royal couple will appear in a multitude of guises and poses. In Barbados Prince Charles is in a T-shirt playing polo, in Fiji he appears as a sailor and in Sierra Leone as a helicopter pilot. Mauritius has chosen to present him in the dress uniform of a Colonel-in-Chief of a Welsh regiment. Such has been the interest in these commemorative issues that Stanley Gibbons, with an admirable spirit of enterprise, have been able to set up a special company to deal ex-

THE CHARLES AND DIANA INDUSTRY

clusively with orders for them.

From the Royal Mint comes a legal tender crown size coin to commemorate the Royal Marriage. The obverse shows Arnold Machin's well known portrait of the Queen, which has appeared on nearly all United Kingdom coinage since 1968 and the reverse features a less formal view of the profiles of Prince Charles and Lady Diana Spencer, designed by Philip Nathan, a freelance sculptor and former Royal Mint engraver. Philip Nathan of Alfold, Surrey was one of six outstanding sculptors invited by the Royal Mint to submit designs. He studied dozens of photographs of Lady Diana before producing the design which was eventually selected by the Royal Mint Advisory Committee and their President, the Duke of Edinburgh, but his labours are not without their reward. The end result will be displayed on five million cupro-nickel crowns struck for circulation.

Proof crowns commemorating events in the United Kingdom are comparatively rare. During the Queen's reign there have only been four previous issues but for the benefit of collectors and investors the Royal Marriage Crown is to appear in a silver proof version, produced in a limited edition of only 250,000.

If the Royal Wedding has provided a much needed injection of life into Britain's business world, it has at the same time provided an opportunity for time-honoured crafts and skills to come to the fore. The Royal School of Needlework have designed an embroidered canvas picture to become a personal memento of the marriage for those whose needlework skills need only extend to a simple tent stitch used throughout and a running stitch for the cross on the dome of St Paul's. Lady Diana's late grandfather the 7th Earl Spencer was a devoted patron of the arts and Chairman of the Royal School of Needlework from 1947 to 1956. During these years he frequently welcomed Royal visitors to Princes Gate, particularly Queen Mary, who was herself an enthusiastic embroiderer, and her daughter-in-law, now the Queen Mother, a much loved patron of the School. Earl Spencer was considered to be quite an accomplished embroiderer and six chair covers of floral-design canvas executed by him are still on view at Althorp in a room occupied in 1913 by King George V and Queen Mary. Appropriately, in designing their canvas picture and a kneeler which also records the Royal Wedding, the Royal School of Needlework have not failed to take into account historical associations.

Of all those involved in the production of souvenirs, the china industry must surely spring most readily to mind. For the industry as a whole the prospect of a Royal

Wedding could not have come at a better time for it has been struck all too obviously by the current economic climate. Aynsley China Ltd in Stoke-on-Trent are justifiably proud of the fact that throughout the present severe recession, the company has been virtually unique in maintaining full-time employment. Aynsley, which was first established in 1775 and is one of the oldest manufacturers in the china industry, is also proud of its long association with Royalty. The company was patronised by Queen Victoria for her residence at Osborne on the

Isle of Wight and subsequently by Queen Mary, Queen Elizabeth the Queen Mother, the late Duchess of Kent and the late Duchess of Gloucester. On the occasion of her marriage to Lieutenant Philip Mountbatten, the Princess Elizabeth chose Aynsley for her wedding china gift from the industry, and in 1981, much to the company's delight, history has repeated itself. From the impressive array of designs submitted to Buckingham Palace by the nation's leading manufacturers, Lady Diana chose "Rosedale" a design of exquisitely executed small

Top *Philip Nathan sculpts the design for the commemorative crown in soft clay. His initial design showed Lady Diana with an attractive windswept quiff of hair but it was thought that this might bring the hair too close to the lettering and that the metal of the hair-line might be too frail. The finished crown above shows her with a fringe, looking more formal beside the smiling Prince.*

English roses portrayed in enamel colours and embellished with coin gold on a highly popular "Crocus" shape. The reaction of the company Chairman was understandably one of pride: "This is the supreme honour for which any manufacturer could wish. It will bring great pride and pleasure to all our employees. Lady Diana has shown perfect taste, her choice echoes the personality and style we would wish of our future Queen." A tankard jug made by John Aynsley, in circa 1793 to record the execution by guillotine of King Louis XVI of France is considered to be one of the oldest commemorative pieces made by an existing china manufacturer and through the years Aynsley have recorded many important occasions with pieces which are retained in collections throughout the world. During the nineteenth century, the company employed a number of highly skilled artists who, working entirely freehand, painted onto fine Bone China subjects of outstanding artistic beauty. The technique is in many ways similar to that of an artist working in oils on canvas, except that in this case enamel colours are used. At each stage

THE CHARLES AND DIANA INDUSTRY

The modelling of the chalice marks an early stage in the production of Aynsley's commemorative piece.

The Wedding Chalice depicts, on an unusual horizontal plane, a scene of Canaerfon Castle.

Terence Abbots works with infinite patience on an Aynsley wall plaque depicting St Paul's Cathedral.

Robert Band, one of four specialists in hand-painting, applies the enamel colours to the Wedding Chalice.

Garrard, The Crown Jewellers, have made their contribution to the commemorabilia in magnificent sterling silver.

Royal Worcester's response to the wedding takes the form of a covered vase, a loving cup and a commemorative plate.

A transfer is applied to the loving cup before it is painted in 22 carat gold.

A honey glazed plate from the Wharf Pottery marks the occasion in hand-thrown slipware.

the piece is fired in special kilns at high temperature to fasten the colour deep into the glaze surface, the process being repeated again and again to achieve the required depth of definition.

Today Aynsley perpetuate the skills introduced during the nineteenth century, in the work of four specialists in hand painting. Under the guidance of Laurence Woodhouse these members of the "Fine Art Division" specialise in the creation of handpainted limited editions and international sporting trophies. It was, they, for example, who

supplied the trophy for the 1981 Grand National and it is they who have been responsible for the fine limited commemorative pieces produced for the marriage of Prince Charles and Lady Diana. The necessary line-drawings for a Wedding Chalice portraying, on an unusual horizontal plane, a hand-painted scene of Caernarfon Castle, and for a Wall Plaque portraying St Paul's Cathedral from across the River Thames, appeared as a remarkably quick response to the engagement announcement. Issued in a certified limited edition of one

hundred and fifty, both the chalice and the plaque were sold out within a matter of weeks and it is a credit to the artistry and the care of those involved in the production of these collectors' items that despite considerable pressure to produce three hundred individually painted commemorative pieces by September, every effort is still made to ensure that the china is not only "individual" (and signed by the artist as a hallmark of authenticity), but also perfect in every respect.

The Royal Worcester Porcelain Company

THE CHARLES AND DIANA INDUSTRY

1,000 metres of silk are reeled from each cocoon in one continuous filament. Each cocoon contains over two miles of silk.

Lullingstone Silk Farm's display shows the rearing and reeling of English silk, used for many Royal occasions, among them the wedding of Princess Elizabeth and Prince Philip.

Choir boys from St Paul's provide the motif which links the four oval tiers.

Frank Weinholt's wedding cake has been specifically designed to show the Prince of Wales' association with Cheshire, as Earl of Chester.

Mulberry leaves are grown with some difficulty, to be consumed by the silkworms as a vital part of the process of sericulture.

The reeling machine reels the silk from each cocoon to produce a strong natural fibre.

When de-gummed, the raw silk becomes soft and lustrous – the perfect fabric for a wedding dress.

is equally proud of its close association with Royalty and the perfection of its commemorative editions. Founded in 1751, it lays claim to a uniquely close and long-lasting link with the Royal Family. In 1788 King George III and Queen Charlotte became the first Royal visitors to the Worcester Porcelain works. The King placed an order for the "Blue Lily" design and granted the company the right to use the style "Manufacturer to their Majesties" and the title "Royal". The design "Blue Lily" was re-named "Royal Lily" and since the

granting of that very first Royal Warrant, Royal Worcester have held Royal Warrants from every succeeding monarch – including Her Majesty Queen Elizabeth II.

About a quarter of a million visitors from Britain and overseas are now welcomed each year at the Royal Porcelain Works, Severn Street, Worcester. In the Dyson Perrins museum they are able to see the finest and most comprehensive historical connection of Royal Worcester porcelain and china in the world. Remarkably, despite increased production facilities, Royal Worcester have

endeavoured to ensure that the same degree of craftmanship, skill and artistry is put into modern products as into their historic counterparts.

The principle that in these days of mass production unique quality work in any art form is, if anything, more highly prized and more widely appreciated is one which underlies the production of limited editions in particular. Since the number of any model is restricted, the very highest standards of artistic and technical skills can be applied to its manufacture. Royal Worcester's answer

THE CHARLES AND DIANA INDUSTRY

to the prospect of a Royal Wedding has taken the form of three very special pieces: a covered vase reminiscent of the famous Imperial Vase made in 1902 for Edward VII and Queen Alexandra, a loving cup hand-painted inside the rim in 22 carat gold, and a commemorative plate featuring portraits of the Royal couple printed from hand-engraved plates.

Garrard, the Crown Jewellers who supplied Lady Diana's engagement ring – a beautiful oval sapphire surrounded by fourteen diamonds and set in 18 carat white gold – have chosen to commemorate the Royal Wedding with a collection of superb sterling silver. Since the company was started by George Wickes a little over 250 years ago a number of significant events have been recorded in silver and following in this historic tradition the wedding of Prince Charles and Lady Diana has been marked with a design intended to capture the romance of the occasion by the use of the Prince of Wales' feathers motif with the C and D initials linked by a true lovers' knot.

If the familiar makers and designers traditionally committed to commemorating historic events have not failed to rise to the occasion then it is all the more interesting to note the relatively new entries into the commemorative field. The name of the potter, Mary Wondrausch was one of only three recommended by the Crafts Council in response to a request by the Dean of St Paul's for someone to produce an official souvenir for the Cathedral. At the Wharf Pottery, 55 St John's Street, Farncombe, Godalming, Surrey, Mary Wondrausch specialises in commemorative plates to celebrate not only a Royal Wedding but every other sort of occasion, be it a birth, a christening or an anniversary. Most of the work is individually commissioned, and it possesses above all, a quality of lively individuality. Mary Wondrausch's absorbing interest in continental peasant art has developed into an overwhelming passion for the English XVIIth century tradition of slipware pottery. The work at the Wharf Pottery is thrown on the wheel in Fremington clay and slipped with Bideford pipe clay and it is a source of justifiable pride that the entire process of producing a plate or pot is performed by hand. Surrounded by a display of traditional pots such as owl jugs, salt kips, egg stands and pitchers, many of them lettered with old potters' sayings, Mary works at her potter's wheel, decorating her wares by trailing her own designs with oxide stained natural clays. By her own admission, her slip-trailers are a source of much amazement. She has designed them herself from "bizarre bicycle inner tubes fixed round corks pierced with empty ballpoint pens and fastened with paper clips". Working with nine different colours at once she admits to feeling and looking like "a sea-lion honking out a tune on old car horns". The entire process, because it is given such undivided personal attention, takes approximately three weeks to complete. The end product is in a seventeenth century tradition but it retains a refreshingly novel quality among the mass-produced Royal Wedding souvenirs.

Not all the souvenir items would fall quite so readily into that difficult category which the Lord Chamberlain is required to define as "good taste". Caught up in the very strongest tide of the souvenir flood the Lord Chamberlain's Office is somehow expected to exercise discreet but decisive control to prevent the "Charles and Diana industry" from running away with itself. Despite the issue of over nine thousand copies of a circular providing guidelines for the production of Royal Wedding commemorabilia and an emphatic statement to the effect that in order to qualify for the privilege of using Royal insignia, the souvenir must be in "good taste", in practice there is little the Lord Chamberlain can do to prevent the Royal insignia from appearing emblazoned on a T-shirt or even on a matching "bra and brief set". "Good taste", at best a matter for subjective judgment, loses all touch with reality when applied to models of the Royal Wedding Coach with plastic corgis trotting along behind it. Of the items submitted to the Design Centre in London in the hope of receiving approval from a committee chaired by Lord Snowdon, something in the region of ninety per cent were rejected. Their rejection does not appear to have reduced sales.

Perhaps after all it is not altogether fair to condemn the Royal Wedding Industry on the grounds of lack of taste or even of commercialism. In an age where cynicism prevails to the extent that it has been suggested that even the date of the engagement announcement was chosen to draw attention away from the disastrous unemployment figures due for release that day, it is not easy to be convinced that there are no sales without demand and that the apparently vast demand reflects a genuine desire to recall a happy and historic occasion. Yet there is a romantic appeal in every wedding and when it is a Royal Wedding that romance assumes a very special mystique. Even the silk from which the wedding dress has been made is not without its particular interest. The famous Lullingstone Silk Farm at Compton House near Sherbourne made the silk for the Coronation robes of King George VI and, among other important Royal orders, they also provided the silk for the train and dress for the wedding of Princess Elizabeth. Lady Diana's wedding ring will be made from a celebrated nugget of Welsh gold which has been kept in the Royal vaults for nearly sixty years. The people of Wales gave it to the Queen Mother for her wedding ring in 1923, and it has since been the source of wedding bands for the Queen, Princess Margaret and Princess Anne. Thus the nugget has become, for as long as it lasts, something of a modern Royal tradition.

Among those selected to use their skills in connection with the event, the obvious delight and sense of privilege belies all cynicism. Included among the wedding cakes to be placed on display at the Wedding Breakfast is the handiwork of Mr Frank Weinholt. The present Mr Weinholt belongs to a line of five generations of confectioners and bakers. He has been a baker for thirty-five years and claims unashamedly that he is "still learning". During those years he has provided not only wedding cakes for Lord and Lady Lichfield and for the Duke and Duchess of Roxborough, but also a christening cake for the Duke and Duchess of Westminster. On the announcement of the Royal engagement he offered his services for the provision of a wedding cake and the offer, much to his delight, was accepted. The design alone of a cake which is five feet high, weighs over 200 lbs and includes 80 lbs marzipan, 40 lbs icing sugar and three bottles of navy rum, took six weeks and numerous sleepless nights. Yet the anxiety was obviously far outweighed by a sense of honour. Such an opportunity is after all, "the peak of any baker's career". The same sentiments were echoed by the wine merchants due to supply the wine for the occasion, and by countless other people, however indirect and tenuous their actual involvement on the day. The more cynical may suggest that David and Elizabeth Emmanuel's delight at receiving the Royal commission for the wedding dress is not entirely uninfluenced by the fact that it has catapulted them to the dizziest heights of the fashion world, but the member of the St John Ambulance Brigade, for whom the opportunity to be on duty on the Royal Wedding route is "the most exciting chance of my lifetime", can have no vested interest.

Since the engagement announcement wedding presents of every conceivable description have poured into Buckingham Palace. One American radio company came to London especially to provide the Royal couple with a traditional American "wedding shower," plans for street parties began immediately and even London Transport have entered into the spirit of the occasion by making plans to gift-wrap their buses. In Central London on the 29th July, the capital's red buses will be dressed up with giant ribbons and bows designed to transform them into "jumbo-sized" wedding presents. At 10 pm on the 28th July the wedding gift from the Household Division takes the form of a firework display in Hyde Park. The background will be a scaffolding firework palace based on the firework display held in Green Park in 1749 to celebrate the peace of Aix-la-Chapelle. The King's troop will fire a gun salute, the massed bands of the Guards Division will play and a torch-lined route for the Royal Party, consisting of Prince Charles, the Queen, Prince Philip and other members of the Royal Family (but not Lady Diana), will be lined by boy scouts.

For the Metropolitan and City Police Forces the need to ensure that the carriage processions pass without interruption on their route from Buckingham Palace, along the Mall, through Trafalgar Square, the Strand, Fleet Street and up Ludgate Hill to St Paul's Cathedral, has meant meticulous planning. The first procession will be for members of the Royal Family accompanied by a captain's escort of the Household Cavalry. The Queen will follow with a sovereign's escort of the Household Cavalry. The Prince of Wales, dressed in full naval

The Mounted Branch of the Metropolitan Police display the skills which enable them to form an essential part of the ceremonial wedding procession. Chief Superintendent Critchlow M.V.O. above and far right is the 'pointer' of the Royal Procession and the five bays seen above are to escort Lady Diana to St Paul's cathedral.

uniform, will arrive with a Prince of Wales' escort of the Household Cavalry and the fourth procession for the bride will be accompanied by a mounted police escort. The occasion carries every promise of justifying its label "Wedding of the Century". Lady Diana Spencer will leave Clarence House for the drive of nearly two miles to the Cathedral in the Glass Coach which has been used for nearly all Royal Weddings since it was built in 1910. The choice reflects a concern that the thousands who flock to London to see the Royal bride should not be

disappointed. Large windows and special interior lighting will provide the crowds with a clear view of the bride. The Queen, it is anticipated, will travel in an open semi-State Landau driven by four grey horses and the Prince of Wales will ride from the Palace in the 1902 State Postillion Landau, specially built for King Edward VII and used by the Queen to meet foreign Heads of State on official visits. Prince Charles and the new Princess will also use this coach on their

return to the Palace. Flags will be flown on the Mall and from Admiralty Arch and members of all three services will line the route and be represented on the Cathedral steps. Eleven static military bands will provide musical accompaniments at various intervals along the processional route.

The organisation of such an occasion has meant close co-operation between a number of different bodies: Buckingham Palace, the Lord Chamberlain's Office, the Metro-

A ROYAL WEDDING

politan and City Police, the London District of the Ministry of Defence (for military arrangements), the Department of the Environment, Westminster City Council and the G.L.C. (granting licences for structures which may need to be built), London Transport, the London Tourist Board, the London Ambulance Service, the London Fire Brigade, St John Ambulance Brigade, the British Transport and the Royal Parks Police – the list is apparently interminable. The real dimensions of the enterprise are immeasurable.

It would be impossible to estimate the size of the crowd which will throng the streets of London to watch the processions on the 29th

George and May Munns, the Pearly King and Queen of East Ham are a traditional part of the London festivities accompanying the Royal Wedding.

Above *The Metropolitan Police motor cycle Special Escort Group provides an escort for Royalty and Heads of State as part of the ceremonial procession.* Right *The Royal Wedding Office at New Scotland Yard was set up specifically to cope with the complex organisation involved in the 'biggest ceremonial event of the century.'*

July but those responsible for the smooth-running of the occasion have worked on the assumption that this will be the most significant ceremonial event of the century. Traffic diversions and road closures will be the most extensive ever. Provision has been made for 3,000-4,000 coaches expected to arrive in London during the night of the 28th/29th, to set down passengers near the processional route and move on to their allotted parking places. Crowds in the Mall are expected to be approximately twenty deep. Every possible eventuality must be

considered – even the guaranteed unpredictability of the English weather. Standby coaches will be available in the event of bad weather and if it rains during the actual ceremony police have prepared a secondary route which will be used to bring closed carriages up to St Paul's and take the open ones away.

The entire route, with the exception of Fleet Street, will be closed from 7 pm on the

previous evening. As a special concession, Fleet Street itself will not be closed until 4 am on the day to allow for the delivery of papers but there will be what the police themselves have described as "a large police presence" in the vicinity of the entire route from the previous day and through the night, to control early arrivals and advise on restrictions. On the 29th July, approximately 2,000 uniformed Metropolitan Police Officers will line the route from Buckingham Palace to Temple Bar, a further 800 City of London Police officers will cover the remainder. Their instructions are to face not the procession but the enthusiastic crowd contained behind the 6,000 steel barriers erected for the occasion. Their function is to "line the route, preserve order, and provide security".

Tragically the necessity for this latter role has been accentuated even in the relatively short interval since the announcement of the Royal engagement. Scattered amongst the lighter Royal Wedding anecdotes, such as that of the ferret expected to pull a nylon chord through a narrow underground duct with a sharply angled bend in order to provide Thames Television with a necessary cable, are the reports of the attempted assassinations of President Reagan and Pope John Paul II, a parcel bomb addressed to the Prince of Wales and an air gun pointed at the Queen during her official birthday celebrations.

The incident involving the Queen as she rode to the Trooping the Colour ceremony cannot fail to emphasise the ultimate inadequacy of any security system. Nevertheless maximum security will be provided. Police officers will be deployed behind the crowd to observe behaviour. Protection officers will be provided as always for all Royalty, visiting Heads of State and British V.I.P.s and the entire route will be monitored on screens linked to twelve closed-circuit television cameras. The television surveillance will be supplemented by physical surveillance at various points along the route. Every building has been vetted. The names of any occupants are known to the police and lists have been compiled of all those who are likely to be present in any given building on the day. Certain buildings, including St Paul's Cathedral will be searched with the assistance of police dogs on the morning of the wedding. Regrettably all this is necessary to ensure that the occasion remains what it should be – an event of unmitigated joy.

It is a tribute to the popularity of Prince Charles and Lady Diana that the rumblings of discontent at the prospect of so splendid a Royal Wedding have been few and faint. The ruling Labour group on North East Derbyshire District Council has decided to fly the red flag from the Council's flagpole on July

29th as "a matter of principle"; the Labour administration of the G.L.C. declined an invitation to the wedding with the gracious comment, "No one elected us to go to weddings. They elected us to try to get the buses running on time", and, according to one councillor of Clay Cross in Derbyshire, when Lady Diana Spencer rides to St Paul's in a glass coach she will also be "riding on the

These pages and previous page *Royal Fireworks 1981. The brilliant burst of some of the many thousand fireworks which heralded the beginning of the Royal Wedding celebrations in Hyde Park on 28 July. Set against a specially constructed Palace façade, the display was watched by 120 distinguished guests, including the British and foreign royal families, and an estimated crowd of over half a million. It included the biggest Catherine Wheel in the world – 40 feet across and spreading fire over a diameter of 100 feet.*

backs of the working class and not realising what a mess the country is in". For the people of Clay Cross, July 29th will be a day of edification, highlighted by some suitably instructive "anti-monarchist plays" explaining to working folk and the unemployed just how wretched and resentful the monarchy ought to make them feel. In general, however, very little criticism has been forthcoming and what little there has been will have come as no surprise to Prince Charles.

"The monarchy", he has said, "is one of the oldest professions in the world" but he has also recognised that "in these times, the monarchy is called into question – it's not to be taken for granted as it used to be. In that sense, one now has to be more professional." Prince Charles' ability to rise to the contemporary challenge has been repeatedly demonstrated. Lady Diana, however, experiencing for the first time the hazards of public life, must still be left wondering how

A ROYAL WEDDING

The night before the morning after! Young and old, determined to catch a glimpse of the superb pageantry that was to follow, work themselves into the spirit of the occasion. In an extravaganza of red, white and blue, people from all over the country, and from abroad, converged on London in Royal Wedding week. For some above a night spent under the stars was sufficient to secure a good vantage point the following day. Others played safe and began camping out two nights before.

A ROYAL WEDDING

it is that her marriage to the man she loves could cause so much suffering.

From the very earliest days of her engagement Lady Diana has made her own distinctive impression on the lifestyle she is now expected to lead. The occasion for her first public appearance with the Prince of Wales was carefully chosen by Buckingham Palace and when Lady Diana stepped out of the Rolls Royce which brought the couple to an evening of verse and music in aid of the Royal Opera House Development Fund, there was little doubt of the success of her debut. In a stunning black dress made from silk taffeta and designed by Elizabeth and

Some people centre *were determined to get some sleep at all costs. For others, any loss of sleep did not deter: the celebrations went on into the night* far right *and everyone seemed as fresh as daisies the following morning* above *and top.*

David Emmanuel, Lady Diana caught the appreciative eyes of the world. The dress took the fashion followers by storm and copies of it were in the shops within forty-eight hours. Mary Quant's verdict was one of unbounded praise: "terrific, absolutely beautiful and so romantic"; and Lady Diana herself was so pleased with the effect that she picked the hitherto unknown Emmanuels to

A ROYAL WEDDING

*Early morning on Royal Wedding Day.
Top Under the kindest of skies and in full view
of the ITV airship, an expectant and patient
crowd watches the comings and goings of the
massed bands as they take up their positions.
Above left Detachments of the Sovereign's
Escort make for Buckingham Palace to take
part in the processions. Above An early
morning toast to the royal couple from the
Society of Toastmasters outside the gates of the
Palace. Left A mass of Press photographers in
position at the foot of the Queen Victoria
Memorial. Opposite page The scene in the
royal park of St James's: flowers, flags and a
colourful contingent of spectators.*

A ROYAL WEDDING

design her wedding dress, in preference to such long-established Royal Dress designers as the House of Hartnell and Ian Thomas. David and Elizabeth Emmanuel have resolved to turn Lady Diana into "a fairy-tale princess" on her wedding day but if the preponderance of "Lady Di look-alikes", "Lady Di haircuts" and general imitators of the "Lady Di look" are any indication, then the Prince of Wales' bride has already captured the imagination and epitomised the secret aspirations of many.

On that very first evening, as Lady Diana made her entrance into the City of London's Goldsmiths' Hall, a member of the waiting crowd stepped forward to offer her a single pink rose. The accompanying card was inscribed with the words "To a lovely lady – an English Rose". The lady in question

As the morning wore on, the crowd's anticipation developed into excitement. Pavements became totally congested above *and the huge corners around Charing Cross began to fill* opposite page. *The whole of the Strand, in front of the Law Courts* top, *for instance, was packed at an early stage. One especially pleasant feature, in an atmosphere of total and intense security, was the attitude of the police who went out of their way to win the confidence and co-operation of a good-humoured crowd.* Far right *Police officers take pictures for the onlookers.* Right *Invitation to the dance.*

Above *Detachment of foot guards leave Buckingham Palace and* right *march to their appointed places in the Mall. Then the Household Brigades emerge to form the head of the royal procession* top.

blushed profusely but it is undoubtedly this image of the fresh, unblemished "English rose" which has appealed to the hearts of even the most critical. There is no doubt either that in the course of time that image will be given the distinctive Royal grooming. However refreshing the giggle, the Royal role may well demand more restraint. Lady Diana is being guided through royal protocol by Prince Charles' former assistant private secretary, Mr Oliver Everett, who has been

perhaps immediately apparent. On 13th March Lady Diana accompanied Prince Charles to Sandown Park. The Queen Mother and Princess Margaret, experienced in the art of race-going, were wisely equipped with sensible flat-heeled shoes but Lady Diana, unprepared, wore court shoes, and as the three walked round the race ring under the close scrutiny of the televison cameras, she must have been painfully aware that her awkward struggles to extricate her heels from the mud were being watched by thousands of potentially critical eyes.

The prospect of a lifetime under constant scrutiny cannot be an altogether easy one. Lady Diana has injected youth, vitality, warmth and a sense of fun into a nation fallen upon hard times and it would be a sad loss if the giggle were to disappear altogether, but her prospective position as third in order of precedence after the Queen and the Queen Mother will demand unmistakable dignity.

Opposite page above *The Queen and Prince Philip head the procession as they emerge from the Palace onto the concourse around the Queen Victoria Memorial* above. *Eight minutes later, Prince Charles and Prince Andrew follow* opposite page below, and right *on their way into the Mall* top and far right. Overleaf *The two brothers and their escort of Life Guards.*

There are already signs that the princess-to-be is learning. A voice from the crowd, calling out "Congratulations, Di" was greeted more recently with a smiling, gentle but nonetheless firm rejoinder: "It's Diana, actually". Prince Charles may call her Di, the Queen may if she wishes, but to the world at large she is, at the very least, Diana. "Humanized" the monarchy may be, but its survival rests upon the nation's need for something romanticised, larger than life and, in some respects at least, removed from the banal reality of ordinary existence. Members of the Royal Family may well be possessed of human emotions and frailties but they are still expected to maintain all the distance, control and style epitomised in the royal wave which Lady Diana has already adopted. The path ahead may be a difficult one and one which may well remove her from the friends and associates of her early years but Lady Diana has remained undaunted. "With Prince Charles beside me," she insists, "I cannot go wrong". If the comment betrays a quiet strength, it is also a timely reminder that a wedding, even a Royal one, is not a meeting of two profiles on

recalled from the British Embassy in Madrid and it is perhaps not altogether insignificant that Lady Diana has been placed in the care of the Queen Mother at Clarence House. There could be no better advisor on the art of becoming Royal, for the Queen Mother knows from personal experience what it means to be thrust from relative obscurity into the forefront of public life. Nothing in the early life of Elizabeth Bowes-Lyon, wife of the Duke of York had tailored her for the requirements of becoming Queen Consort but the respect and popularity which she still commands bears witness to her proficiency in the art of royal behaviour.

The ground rules may be simple but not

A ROYAL WEDDING

a souvenir plate, an event designed to boost trade or upset Labour councillors but the sealing of a relationship born of love. The event which will take place in St Paul's Cathedral on 29th July will be an historic occasion, witnessed by millions, and bearing with it a sense of tradition and continuity, of the past carried forward into the present and joyously projected into the future, but it must remain at the same time a very special and unique occasion for two individuals committing their lives to each other.

───── ♔ ─────

The choice of venue for the marriage ceremony represents a break with tradition but it also reflects the couple's personal choice. Traditionally it is Westminster Abbey with its close historical relationship with Royalty and Parliament which provides the setting for Royal Weddings. Yet St Paul's

Opposite page *The bridegroom's procession nears the end of the drive to St Paul's as the 1902 State Landau carries Prince Charles up Ludgate Hill.* Above and above right *The Queen and Prince Philip in an open semi-State landau. Other royal guests included Princess Anne and Princess Margaret* top, *and Prince and Princess Michael of Kent* right.

stands on equally hallowed and historic ground, for on the summit of Ludgate Hill a Christian church has stood for more than 1,300 years. The present great masterpiece is one of a number of buildings which have stood on this site and borne the name of London's patron saint. The Anglo-Saxons built a cathedral on the site in AD604, the

Normans rebuilt it and by the end of the Middle Ages, it had become one of the largest Gothic churches in Europe. After its destruction by the Great Fire of London in 1666 it was rebuilt by Sir Christopher Wren and completed in 1708, miraculously to survive the destruction of the Second World War. Internally, as externally, Wren's "new" cathedral is dominated by a dome, the height and dimensions of which, lend the building an air of spaciousness and light.

St Paul's is not without its Royal Associations. In 1789 King George III went to the Cathedral to thank God for his deliverance from illness and in 1897 it was here that Queen Victoria attended a thanksgiving service to mark her Jubilee. She was too infirm to mount the steps to the building

A ROYAL WEDDING

Top *An advance procession of Service Chiefs heads past the Law Courts in the Strand.* Opposite page above *A celebratory banner on Blackfriars Bridge proclaims London's good wishes to Prince Charles and his bride. A complete view of the bridegroom's carriage procession* opposite page below *shows the four Oldenburg Greys with their impressive silver mane-dressings.* Above *Lady Diana Spencer, swathed in a mass of ivory tulle, joins the procession in the Glass Coach.* Left *Her coach being drawn up Ludgate Hill.*

A ROYAL WEDDING

itself and so the service was held outside and the Queen never left her carriage. In 1977 it was to St Paul's that Queen Elizabeth II came to give thanks for her Silver Jubilee and when the Queen Mother celebrated her eightieth birthday it was understandably amongst the splendour and majesty of the cathedral of which she is patron.

The choice of St Paul's as opposed to Westminster Abbey has been attributed to the fact that the cathedral can hold several hundred more guests. Two thousand five hundred people have been invited to attend the wedding ceremony and still Buckingham Palace is compelled to admit: "Unfortunately some people are being disappointed" ..."More than 2,500 places may

seem like a lot for a wedding but when you try to spread them out over the world, and try to represent the various sections of the community, it ends up with being too few." The more open, accessible design of St Paul's also possesses advantages which even the far-sighted Sir Christopher Wren could not have foreseen. Vision, unimpeded by the screen which in the mediaeval Abbey separates the choir and the clergy from the congregation, is considered an unquestionable asset in modern technological terms and, over and above such empirical considerations, the building's primary function must not be forgotten. To the Very Reverend Alan Webster, the Dean of St Paul's, who will assist the Archbishop of Canterbury in conducting the service, the Cathedral's open dimensions speak of the fact that St Paul's is "the people's church". "Wren was a vicar's kid and a religious man who believed that God was light. He was also a seventeenth-century man who conceived his masterpiece in the spirit of his day. This is a church where men and women can relate directly to God. The Cathedral was built for God. It exists for everybody."

The Dean and Chapter of four canons, whose collective word is law within the Cathedral precincts, were delighted at the choice of St Paul's. The news inevitably

Far left *The Duchess of Gloucester and her mother-in-law, Princess Alice, are driven to St Paul's in a State Landau.* Top *The Queen Mother, wearing cool blue-green, is escorted by her youngest grandson, Prince Edward. Princess Alexandra and her husband, the Hon. Angus Ogilvy, were also in the procession* left *with their children, James and Marina.* Above *The Queen and the Duke of Edinburgh wave as they reach the end of their journey.* Opposite page *Splendid views of the bridegroom's mounted escort and of the Prince of Wales' carriage and outriders as they near the Cathedral.*

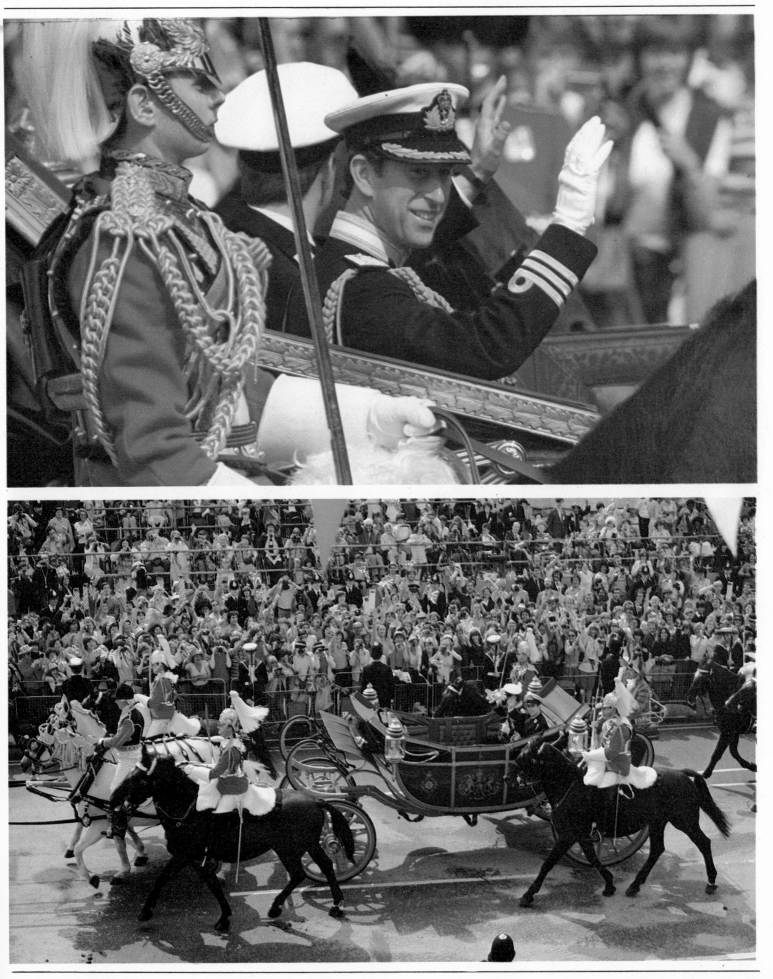

A ROYAL WEDDING

Top left *Chief bridesmaids India Hicks and Lady Sarah Armstrong Jones, who is seen* above *following the bride into St Paul's.* Top *The Queen and Queen Mother turn to wave as they enter the Cathedral with Prince Philip and Prince Edward.* Left *Lady Diana turns to check that all is well as she ascends the steps. The pictures* opposite *show the early arrival of the bridesmaids* right, *and the beginning of Lady Diana's long walk up the nave on the arm of her father* top *and* bottom *followed by her attendants* centre.

created additional pressures. When a Prince of Wales marries then even the administration of St Paul's becomes only one more cog in the wheel of State. Yet the reaction from the whole Cathedral staff appears to have been one of pleasure. They are obviously well used to the pressure of conducting the religious life of a Cathedral where attendance of the main services on Sundays is estimated at between 1,000 and 2,000, in the full glare of publicity, and this pressure must not be allowed to detract from St Paul's spiritual role. In the midst of all the purely practical preparations for a dynastic event

the Dean is still concerned that St Paul's "should not simply be an immense building but a place of the Spirit", and the distinct impression remains that whilst he is by no means oblivious to the historic and public implications of the occasion, he is still very much concerned with the marriage of two young people.

The initiative in the wedding preparations, the Dean insists, has come very much from the Prince of Wales and his bride. The

A ROYAL WEDDING

2,500 invited guests will include amongst their number personal friends of the couple such as Colonel and Camilla Parker-Bowles, Prince Charles' skiing companion, Charlie Palmer Tomkinson, actress Susan George, Lady Diana's former flatmates, and almost certainly the six girls tipped to become Ladies-in-Waiting – Lady Jane Spencer, Lady Penelope Romsey, Lady Dale Tryon, Rowena Brassey, Victoria Legge Bourke and Lady Joanna Knatchbull.

Prince Charles' two "supporters" who traditionally replace the role of best man will be his two brothers – Prince Andrew who will carry the ring, and Prince Edward. The five bridesmaids will include, at Lady Diana's express request, one of the children from the Pimlico nursery school – five-year-old Clementine Hambro, a great-granddaughter of Sir Winston Churchill. The other bridesmaids will be Lady Sarah Armstrong-Jones, India Hicks, Sarah Jane Gaselee, daughter of Prince Charles' racing trainer and Catherine Cameron, daughter of two close friends of the Prince of Wales. Lord Nicholas Windsor, youngest son of the Duke and Duchess of Kent, and Edward van Cutsem will be the pages.

The music for the occasion is a traditional English blend chosen very largely by Prince Charles and the service itself represents a break with tradition. It follows the Series I Alternative Marriage Rite of the Church of England which permits the bride to exclude the promise to obey her husband. The presence and participation of representatives of a number of Churches will make it a more ecumenical service than any previous Royal Wedding. Apart from Dr Runcie, Cardinal Basil Hume, Roman Catholic Archbishop of Westminster and the Right Rev. Andrew Doig, Moderator of the General Assembly of the Church of Scotland will read the prayers. Mr George Thomas, Speaker of the House of Commons and a leading Methodist will read the first lesson. The Dean of St Paul's has understandably referred to the fact that the service will represent "the drawing together of the churches" and so yet another dimension has been added to an occasion

which marks, above all, the birth of a new human relationship.

The vision emerges of an event endowed with interest and importance at many different and apparently conflicting levels: historical and contemporary, commercial and spiritual, public and personal. Yet the momentous but somehow simple ceremony which will take place before the eyes of the world in the "people's church" bears with it the unspoken offer of a perhaps unprecedented "drawing together". The words of the wedding service itself speak more eloquently than any others of the true significance of the occasion…

The superbly rich splendour of the interior of St Paul's matches the historic occasion as right *Lady Diana, dressed in ivory silk with a veil and train spangled with mother-of-pearl and sequins, follows the clergy towards the Choir.* Top *She approaches the specially constructed platform, which effectively extends the chancel, and at which Prince Charles waits with his supporters Prince Andrew and Prince Edward. Having reached this point, she stands before the Archbishop of Canterbury* opposite page *with her father on her left and her husband-to-be on her right.*

A ROYAL WEDDING

At the day and time appointed for solemnization of Matrimony, the persons to be married shall come into the body of the Church with their friends and neighbours: and there standing together, the Man on the right hand and the Woman on the left, THE DEAN *shall say,*

DEARLY beloved, we are gathered here in the sight of God and in the face of this congregation, to join this man and this woman in Holy Matrimony; which is an honourable estate instituted by God himself, signifying unto us the mystical union that is betwixt Christ and his Church; which holy estate Christ adorned and beautified with his presence, and first miracle that he wrought, in Cana of Galilee, and is commended in Holy Writ to be honourable among all men; and therefore is not by any to be enterprised, nor taken in hand, unadvisedly, lightly, or wantonly; but reverently, discreetly, soberly, and in the fear of God, duly considering the causes for which Matrimony was ordained.

First, It was ordained for the increase of mankind according to the will of God, and that children might be brought up in the fear and nurture of the Lord, and to the praise of his Holy name.

Secondly, It was ordained in order that the natural instincts and affections, implanted by God, should be hallowed and directed aright; that those who are called of God to this holy estate, should continue therein in pureness of living.

Thirdly, It was ordained for the mutual society, help and comfort, that the one ought to have of the other, both in prosperity and adversity.

Into which holy estate these two persons present come now to be joined.

Therefore if any man can shew any just cause, why they may not lawfully be joined together, let him now speak, or else hereafter for ever hold his peace.

Then, speaking unto the persons that shall be married, THE ARCHBISHOP OF CANTERBURY *shall say,*

Opposite *The rich warm light of the interior of St Paul's, as the Prince and Lady Diana stand at the chancel steps before the Dean at the beginning of the service, evidences the wisdom of the decision to hold the wedding at the Cathedral rather than at Westminster Abbey.* Top *The Queen, Prince Philip, the Queen Mother, Princess Anne, Captain Phillips, Princess Margaret and Viscount Linley wait for the bride to arrive.* Centre and below *Two almost simultaneous views of the solemnization of the marriage: the Archbishop of Canterbury gives his blessing as the bride and groom kneel before him.*

I REQUIRE and charge you both, as ye will answer at the dreadful day of judgment when the secrets of all hearts shall be disclosed, that if either of you know any impediment, why ye may not be lawfully joined together in Matrimony, ye do now confess it. For be ye well assured, that so many as are coupled together otherwise than God's word doth allow are not joined together by God; neither is their Matrimony lawful.

If no impediment be alleged, then shall the Archbishop say unto the Man,

CHARLES PHILIP ARTHUR GEORGE, wilt thou have this woman to thy wedded wife, to live together after God's ordinance in the holy estate of Matrimony? Wilt thou love her, comfort her, honour, and keep her, in sickness and in health; and, forsaking all other, keep thee only unto her, so long as ye both shall live?

The Man shall answer, I will

Then shall the Archbishop say unto the Woman,

Far right *With the Prince and his bride now married, the first part of the wedding ceremony is over and the royal couple sit for an address by the Archbishop. Then, during the singing of Parry's anthem "I Was Glad" they rise* right *and follow the Archbishop to the High Altar for prayers* above. Opposite *Another superb view of a significant point in the service: the Prince and Princess stand before the Altar, which is fashioned in Sicilian marble and overhung by the huge ornate cupola bearing the figure of Christ in Majesty.* Top *After the signing of the Register, the newly married couple walk back down the nave towards the West door of the Cathedral.*

DIANA FRANCES, wilt thou have this man to thy wedded husband, to live together according to God's law in the holy estate of Matrimony? Wilt thou love him, comfort him, honour and keep him, in sickness and in health; and, forsaking all other, keep thee only unto him, so long as ye both shall live?

The Woman shall answer, I will

Then shall the Archbishop say, Who giveth this Woman to be married to this Man?

Then shall they give their troth to each other in this manner.

The Archbishop, receiving the Woman at her father's hands, shall cause the Man with his right hand to take the Woman by her right hand, and to say after him as followeth.

I, CHARLES PHILIP ARTHUR GEORGE take thee DIANA FRANCES to my wedded wife, to have and to hold from this day forward, for better for worse, for richer for poorer, in sickness and in health, to love and to cherish, till death us do part, according to God's holy ordinance; and thereto I plight thee my troth.

Then shall they loose their hands; and the Woman, with her right hand taking the Man by his right hand, shall likewise say after the Archbishop,

I DIANA FRANCES take thee CHARLES PHILIP ARTHUR GEORGE to my wedded husband, to have and to hold from this day forward, for better for worse, for richer for poorer, in sickness and in health, to love and to cherish, till death us do part, according to God's holy law; and thereto I give thee my troth.

Then shall they again loose their hands; and the Man shall give unto the Woman a ring, laying the same upon the book. And the Archbishop shall say a prayer for the blessing of the ring.

BLESS, O LORD this ring, and grant that he who gives it and she who shall wear it may remain faithful to each other, and abide in thy peace and favour, and live together in love until their lives' end. Through Jesus Christ our Lord. *Amen.*

Then the Archbishop, taking the ring, shall deliver it unto the Man to put it upon the fourth finger of the Woman's left hand. And the Man, holding the ring there, and taught by the Archbishop, shall say,

WITH this ring I thee wed; with my body I thee honour; and all my worldly goods with thee I share: In the name of the Father, and of the Son, and of the Holy Ghost. *Amen.*

Then the Man leaving the ring upon the fourth finger of the Woman's left hand, they shall both kneel down: the congregation shall remain standing, and the Archbishop shall say, Let us pray

O ETERNAL GOD, Creator and Preserver of all

The moment the crowds outside the Cathedral, and the several hundred million throughout the world who watched the wedding on television, had waited for – the first public appearance of Britain's new Princess of Wales on the arm of her husband. Top *The bride's triumphant wave to the wildly cheering crowds.* Right and opposite *Both partners radiating happiness as they descend the steps towards their waiting carriage.*

A ROYAL WEDDING

mankind, giver of all spiritual grace, the author of everlasting life; Send thy blessing upon these thy servants, this man and this woman, whom we bless in thy name; that, living faithfully together, they may surely perform and keep the vow and covenant betwixt them made, whereof this ring given and received is a token and pledge; and may ever remain in perfect love and peace together, and live according to thy laws; through Jesus Christ our Lord. *Amen.*

Then shall the Archbishop join their right hands together, and say, Those whom God hath joined together let no man put asunder.

Then shall the Archbishop speak unto the people.

FORASMUCH as CHARLES PHILIP ARTHUR GEORGE *and* DIANA FRANCES have consented together in holy wedlock, and have witnessed the same before God and this company, and thereto have given and pledged their troth to each other, and have declared the same by giving and receiving of a ring,

Opposite page *Almost the whole of the interior of St Paul's is in view as Prince Charles and his wife begin their progress from the Dean's Aisle, through the choir and nave, to the steps of the Cathedral.* Top *The end of that progress, and Prince and Princess take their leave of the clergy who participated in the 1¼ hour-long service.* Above right *Now settled in the 1902 State Landau, pulled by the four Greys which took Prince Charles to the wedding, they prepare for a tumultuous drive back to Buckingham Palace where they arrived* above *shortly before one o'clock.* Right *The mother of the groom travels with the father of the bride: the Queen and Earl Spencer leave St Paul's.*

and by joining of hands; I pronounce that they be man and wife together, In the name of the Father, and of the Son, and of the Holy Ghost. *Amen.*

And the Archbishop shall add this Blessing.

GOD the Father, God the Son, God the Holy Ghost, bless, preserve, and keep you; the Lord mercifully with his favour look upon you; and so fill you with all spiritual benediction and grace, that ye may so live together in this life, that in the world to come ye may have life everlasting. *Amen.*

A ROYAL WEDDING

Then shall all be seated, and the Choirs of St Paul's Cathedral and Her Majesty's Chapels Royal shall sing the following anthem.

Let the people praise thee, O God: yea, let all the people praise thee.

O let the nations rejoice and be glad: for thou shalt judge the folk righteously, and govern the nations upon earth.

Then shall the earth bring forth her

increase: and God, even our own God, shall give us his blessing.

God shall bless us: and all the ends of the world shall fear him.

God be merciful unto us, and bless us: and shew us the light of his countenance, and be merciful unto us.

That thy way may be known upon earth: thy saving health among all nations.

Glory be to the Father, and to the Son: and to the Holy Ghost;

As it was in the beginning, is now, and ever shall be: world without end. *Amen.*

From Psalm 67   *William Mathias*

The long journey back to Buckingham Palace for the Prince and Princess of Wales was accompanied by a continuous and tumultous roar of delight from the crowd. These photographs show how pleased the new Princess was with the warmth of her reception as the royal couple's procession left the precincts of St Paul's Cathedral. They were driven in the 1902 State Postillion Landau in which Prince Charles and Prince Andrew had ridden to the service.

A ROYAL WEDDING

Then shall follow the Lesson, read by THE RIGHT HONOURABLE GEORGE THOMAS, SPEAKER OF THE HOUSE OF COMMONS: *the Thirteenth Chapter of the First Epistle of St Paul to the Corinthians.*

All shall remain seated for the Address by THE MOST REVEREND AND RIGHT HONOURABLE ROBERT RUNCIE, MC, DD, ARCHBISHOP OF CANTERBURY, PRIMATE OF ALL ENGLAND AND METROPOLITAN.

Then the Choirs shall sing the following anthem.

I WAS glad when they said unto me, we will go into the house of the Lord. Our feet shall stand in thy gates, O Jerusalem. Jerusalem is builded as a city that is at unity in itself.

O pray for the peace of Jerusalem, they shall prosper that love thee. Peace be within

Top left *A wave from Prince Charles and his Princess as their carriage leaves the Cathedral steps.* Left and above left *The Queen drives back with Earl Spencer.* Far left *Princess Alexandra and her family;* top *Prince and Princess Michael of Kent leave St Paul's;* while the Queen Mother is now accompanied by Prince Andrew above. Opposite page *The Queen with Earl Spencer, and Prince Philip with Mrs Shand-Kydd.*

thy walls, and plenteousness within thy palaces.

Psalm 122: 1-3, 6, 7
Charles Hubert Hastings Parry

The anthem ended, the congregation shall kneel for the Prayers.

A ROYAL WEDDING

The Lesser Litany Versicles and Responses shall be sung by the Minor Canon and the Choirs.

Lord, have mercy upon us
Christ, have mercy upon us
Lord, have mercy upon us

V. O Lord, save thy servant, and thy handmaid;
R. Who put their trust in thee.

V. O Lord, send them help from thy holy place;
R. And evermore defend them.

V. Be unto them a tower of strength;
R. From the face of their enemy.

V. O Lord, hear our prayer;
R. And let our cry come unto thee.

Christopher Dearnley

Then THE RIGHT REVEREND AND RIGHT HONOURABLE THE LORD COGGAN *shall say,*

HEAVENLY FATHER, we thank you that in our early lives you speak to us of our eternal life: we pray that through their marriage CHARLES *and* DIANA may know you more clearly, love you more dearly, and follow you more nearly, day by day; through Jesus Christ our Lord, *Amen.*

THE CARDINAL ARCHBISHOP OF WESTMINSTER *shall say,*

ALMIGHTY GOD, you send your Holy Spirit to be the life and light of all your people. Open the hearts of these your children to the riches of his grace, that they may bring forth the fruit of the Spirit in love and joy and peace; through Jesus Christ our Lord. *Amen.*

THE MODERATOR OF THE GENERAL ASSEMBLY OF THE CHURCH OF SCOTLAND *shall say,*

HEAVENLY FATHER, maker of all things, you enable us to share in your work of creation. Bless this couple in the gift and care of children, that their home may be a place of love, security, and truth, and their children grow up to know and love you in your Son, Jesus Christ our Lord. *Amen.*

THE REVEREND HARRY WILLIAMS *shall say,*

O GOD, you who are the giver of all happiness because you are the giver of all love, we thank you and praise your name for the love you have given to these your servants CHARLES PRINCE OF WALES and DIANA PRINCESS OF WALES. Bless and enrich them in their joy; grant that they may continually grow in their understanding and support of one another so that their home may be to them a sanctuary

Top *Queen Elizabeth the Queen Mother and Prince Andrew.* Far left *The Duke and Duchess of Kent with their elder son, the Earl of St Andrew's, and their daughter, Lady Helen Windsor.* Above *Princess Margaret and her niece, Princess Anne.* Left *A bird's eye view into the bride's carriage.* Opposite page *The Prince and Princess of Wales crossing Ludgate Circus.*

where they may ever be made new; supply them with the resources they will need to meet the great responsibilities which will fall upon them in their life of service to this kingdom and commonwealth; and when, as all people must, they have to go through times of hardship and trial, give them the wisdom and strength to bring them through victoriously. We thank you for all they mean to us and will do for us. And, as we rejoice in their happiness, grant us all to see that it is in

A ROYAL WEDDING

the service of your self-giving love alone that true happiness can be found, as was shown by your Son, Jesus Christ our Lord. *Amen.*

Then shall he lead the congregation in saying,

OUR FATHER, who art in heaven, Hallowed be thy Name. Thy Kingdom come. Thy will be done, on earth as it is in heaven. Give us this day our daily bread. And forgive us our trespasses. As we forgive those who trespass against us. And lead us not into temptation; But deliver us from evil. *Amen.*

And continue with the Blessing of the Couple.

ALMIGHTY GOD, the Father of our Lord Jesus Christ, Pour upon you the riches of his grace, sanctify and bless you, that you may please him both in body and soul, and live together in holy love unto your lives' end.

The congregation standing, all shall sing the following hymn.

I VOW to thee, my country, all earthly
    things above,
Entire and whole and perfect, the service of
    my love:
The love that asks no question, the love that
    stands the test,
That lays upon the altar the dearest and
    the best;
The love that never falters, the love that
    pays the price,

Opposite page above *An uncharacteristic view of a section of the 650,000 spectators lining the route as they wait patiently for the procession to pass.* Above *A respite for police and mounted militia before the Royal Family returns from St Paul's.* Top *The carriage bearing the Duke of Edinburgh and Mrs Peter Shand-Kydd.* Centre right *Salutes and cheers for the Queen Mother as she passes by St Clement Danes. Her carriage is followed by the landau in which Princess Margaret, Princess Anne, Captain Mark Phillips and Viscount Linley ride* right, *travelling towards St Mary-in-the-Strand.* Opposite page below *Sarah Gaselee and Clementine Hambro enjoying their ride back in Queen Alexandra's State Coach.* Overleaf *Bride, groom and well-wishers.*

A ROYAL WEDDING

The love that makes undaunted the final
sacrifice.

And there's another country, I've heard of
long ago,
Most dear to them that love her, most great
to them that know;
We may not count her armies, we may not
see her King;
Her fortress is a faithful heart, her pride
is suffering;
And soul by soul and silently her shining
bounds increase,
And her ways are ways of gentleness and all
her paths are peace.

Cecil Spring-Rice　　　　　*Gustav Holst*

All shall kneel and THE ARCHBISHOP OF CAN-
TERBURY *shall pronounce the Blessing.*

GOD the Holy Trinity make you strong in
faith and love, defend you on every side, and
guide you in truth and peace; and the blessing of God Almighty, the Father, the Son,
and the Holy Spirit, be among you and
remain with you always.

Amen　　　　　*Orlando Gibbons*

All shall stand to sing

GOD save our gracious Queen,
Long live our noble Queen,
God save the Queen.
Send her victorious,

*The exultant new girl on the balcony – Diana,
Princess of Wales, in relaxed mood* far left *as
she and her husband acknowledge the
persistent acclamations from below.* Top *Bride
and groom with something to smile about.*
Above *The moment nobody anticipated –
probably the first balcony kiss in history.* Left
*A pensive Princess of Wales surveys the scene as
almost three quarters of a million people surge
towards the Palace.* Opposite *The happiest
wave of the year. For the first time since 1863,
Britain welcomed a new Princess of Wales –
and with unreserved delight.*

A ROYAL WEDDING

Happy and glorious,
Long to reign over us:
God save the Queen.

Thy choicest gifts in store
On her be pleased to pour,
Long may she reign.
May she defend our laws,
And ever give us cause
To sing with heart and voice,
God save the Queen.

Arranged by David Willcocks

Then shall the Archbishop of Canterbury precede the Bride and Bridegroom to the Dean's Aisle for the signing of the Register.

Jubilant balcony scenes as the bride and groom appear opposite page above *with their bridesmaids and pages – from left to right, India Hicks, Edward van Cutsem, Clementine Hambro, Lord Nicholas Windsor, Sarah Gaselee, Lady Sarah Armstrong Jones and Catherine Cameron.* Top left and opposite page below *The Queen joins her son and daughter-in-law.* Above *Lord Spencer and the Queen at the side of the bride and groom.* Left *A close-up of the newly-married couple.* Far left *Alone on the balcony, the Prince and Princess wave as* overleaf *the vast crowd cheers ecstatically.*

A ROYAL WEDDING

Above *Lord Lichfield's formal photograph showing the bride and groom, their bridesmaids and pages, with members of all the reigning royal families of Europe except Spain. From left to right: King Carl XVI of Sweden, Prince Henrik of Denmark, Queen Silvia of Sweden, Queen Margrethe of Denmark, King Baudouin of the Belgians, King Olav of Norway, James Ogilvy, Queen Fabiola of the Belgians, Marina Ogilvy, Princess Margaret, Captain Mark Phillips, Princess Anne, Angus Ogilvy, Princess Alexandra, the Queen Mother, Prince Andrew, Viscount Linley, the Duchess of Gloucester, Prince Philip, the Queen, the Duke of Gloucester, Prince Edward, Princess Alice of Gloucester, the Duke of Kent, Ruth, Lady Fermoy, the Earl of St Andrew's, Mrs Shand-Kydd, the Duchess of Kent, Viscount Althorp, Lady Jane Fellowes, Earl Spencer, Anthony Fellowes, Prince Michael, Lady Sarah McCorquodale, Princess Michael, Neil McCorquodale, Queen Beatrix of the Netherlands, Princess Grace of Monaco, Prince Claus of the Netherlands, Prince Albert of Monaco, Lady Helen Windsor, Princess Gina of Liechtenstein, Grand Duke Jean of Luxembourg, Prince Franz-Josef of Liechtenstein and Grand Duchess Josephine-Charlotte of Luxembourg.* Left *A classic study of the Princess of Wales with her sweeping ivory tulle train.* Opposite *The 21st Prince of Wales and his Princess – another formal portrait by the Earl of Lichfield.* Overleaf *Serious husband with serene wife – Prince Charles in naval uniform and the Princess in her magnificent wedding dress and tiara.*

A ROYAL WEDDING

During the Procession shall be played the March from the Overture to the Occasional Oratorio by George Frideric Handel.

The Dean and Chapter with the Bishop of London will conduct Her Majesty The Queen, His Royal Highness The Prince Philip, Duke of Edinburgh, and those who are to sign the Register to the Dean's Aisle.

During the signing of the Register, there shall be sung, by Miss Kiri Te Kanawa and The Bach Choir with Mr John Wallace (trumpet) and orchestra, an Aria and Chorus from Samson by George Frideric Handel.

LET the bright Seraphim in burning row,
Their loud uplifted angel-trumpets blow;
Let the Cherubic host, in tuneful choirs
Touch their immortal harps with
  golden wires.

Let their celestial concerts all unite,
Ever to sound his praise in endless morn of
light.

After the signing of the Register a Fanfare shall be sounded and the orchestra shall play

Pomp and Circumstance March No. 4 in G
Edward Elgar
Crown Imperial
William Walton

The high nervous tension of the wedding ceremony now well past, the balcony appearances over, the official photographs taken, and the speeches made, the Prince and Princess faced the final public ordeal of their great day. With a honeymoon about to begin at Broadlands, the couple left Buckingham Palace at 4.30 pm to ride in an open State Landau to Waterloo Station where a train would be waiting to take them to Romsey. These pictures right show their progress out of the Palace and into the Mall at the start of that journey. Above The relaxed and happy couple – a picture of contentment – as they begin their new life as man and wife.

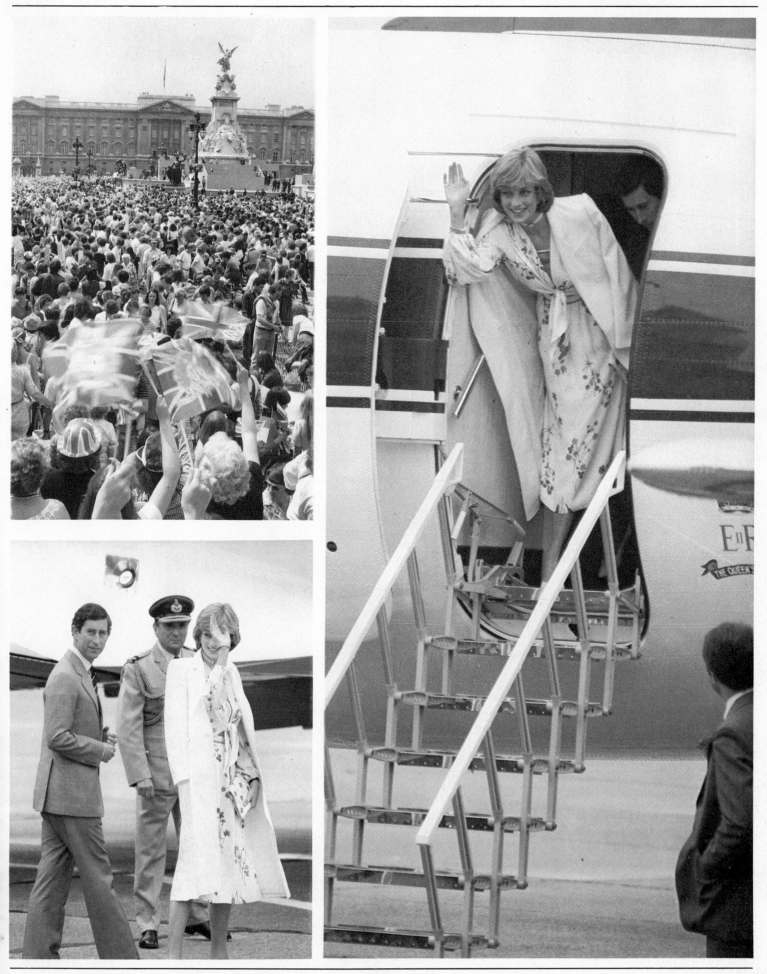

THE HONEYMOON

THE HONEYMOON

THE HONEYMOON